People Are Saying ...

Present Truth For a New Generation

As I read through the first few chapters, my heart leapt because this is one of the Greatest Events in the History of the world. Jeanne Halsey has a unique way of bringing present truth out of this miraculous event: Jesus as my personal Passover Lamb! The Ultimate Sacrifice bringing God's peace back to the Earth!

God bless you big, Jeanne, as you bring forth this ancient truth for a whole new generation of believers. May God continue to grace you as He uses you to open up this awesome event, showing why it is so vitally important in this hour. It seems like many things in our age gets watered down, but this book brings us back to one of the most powerful events in the history of the world.
~ **Rev. Darcy Dubé;** Senior Pastor, *Destiny Church,* Tsawwassen, British Columbia, Canada

Teaching Truth Through Story-Telling

Our whole family studied this carefully, and our children especially liked the ongoing saga of "Charlie the Angel" – you are a great story-teller! Teaching Bible truths through story-telling is an excellent concept (Jesus did it too, via the Parables). We are changing our phrasing to the *"Season of the Lamb"* as a result of this book.
~ **Gloria Edwards,** mother of five; Salem, Oregon

BEHOLD THE LAMB

An Easter Bible Study

By Jeanne Gossett Halsey

BEHOLD THE LAMB

An Easter Bible Study

By **Jeanne Gossett Halsey**

ISBN 978-1-300-92545-3

For more information, contact:

ReJoyce Books
4424 Castlerock Drive
Blaine, Washington 98230
United States of America

360.332.5080

www.halseywrite.com

In honor of **Joyce
Aletha** *née*
**Shackelford
Gossett;**
1929-1991

Table of Contents

Day 6 (Good Friday): D-Day

Day 7 (Saturday): What **Really** Was Going On?

Day 8 (Lamb's Sunday): Alive Forevermore

Foreword: "Yesterday and Today"
By Reba Rambo-McGuire

I had never seen anything like it: a family Bible study/prayer, with chips and dips, shorts and tee-shirts ... and Mama Joyce presiding in a flowered caftan.

My best friend Judy Gossett had invited me home with her to Blaine, Washington, for a visit with her family. Of course, I had heard many stories about her famous father: minister, mission-ary and author, the Rever-end Don Gossett ... and her effervescent mother Joyce. Judy had reminis-ced about countless antics between the five Gossett siblings, so I expected a colorful tribe – but nothing quite prepared me for that first evening at their home, especially when I learned there would be a gathering for chicken tacos and stimu-lating conversation disguised as a Bible study!

At 18 years of age, the few boring home Bible studies I had attended in our little coal-mining community were rigid: red-letter Bible, pens and paper in hand ... like Marines at a strategic military training base. There was usually the typical in-structor who expounded in a matter-of-fact, dry-as-cardboard and long-as-the-last-day-of-school manner. Sitting there in the Gossett family living room was anything but typical, dry and boring.

Picture this: Don (whom I quickly learned to call "Padre") Gossett, in his short-sleeved, *"I just got off the plane from the Philippines"* shirt, munching on a jar of peanuts and talking between chews about the power of words ... Donnie (the youngest brother) grinning like a Cheshire cat, strumming on a guitar and scribbling a lyric ... Judy (the oldest sister) kneeling on the shag rug by the orange leather ottoman – not praying, just being "Judy who kneels" ... Jeanne (the middle sister) curled up in a lotus position, stringing beads on some sort of hippie-looking necklace ... Michael (the oldest brother) being a Jesus-look-alike with long hair and faded jeans ... little Marisa (the baby sister) sucking on a huge lollipop while coloring pictures intently ... and "Joyce My Choice," as they affectionately called her, floating around, pouring cream sodas, replenishing bowls of popcorn, and interrupting whoever and whenever she pleased.

Of course, I – the visitor from Planet Kentucky – had pencil poised, back rigid and, as my Granny used to say, "My ears on."

I had never experienced a family who had so many opinions! It was like a tennis match with the ball lobbying back and forth between seven play-ers. I wouldn't call it arguing – it was a rare and lively interchange between family members who actually listened, weighed and respected the viewpoints of all participating.

Often they would segue into a funny story, or Donnie would crack a joke and then Michael would top it. The amazing thing was the sense that there was nothing unimportant, trivial or taboo. I blushed more than once at their openness and range of subjects. It was the most honest, straightforward and informative conversation I had ever observed in a Christian home. Even when there were polar-opposite opinions, somehow they agreed to disagree and still be family.

At some point I realized we had transitioned from studying to praying. In Walnut Grove, Kentucky, praying was serious business, and we had always shut our eyes tight (*"with every head bowed, every eye closed and nobody looking around"*). But in that room, I learned to **watch and pray.** At first I didn't quite know what to do with that – but glancing over at Judy, still kneeling yet also coloring a picture of Minnie Mouse as she prayed, somehow it felt suddenly right.

Understand: their prayers were intense and sincere, but there was no fear of rejection or condemnation. It was liberating! I had never heard so many Scriptures prayed out loud before. Wow, what a concept: pray the Word!

I was also amazed to experience an entire family who communicated with such an extensive and comprehensive vocabulary. I'd been a voracious reader since I was 5, and had a substantial grasp of language – but I learned the hard way in my beloved hills: if you use big words, you will be accused of being a show-off who thinks you're better than everyone else. I had such a fear of rejection in school, I had learned to minimize my words ... except on the pages of my locked diary.

Miraculously – in that living room, through the experience of a family simply being who they were – I was being healed of wounds and distorted paradigms. I was free to speak a dialect for every man and culture ... the simple and the profound. Through the power of Holy Spirit, I could speak a language for all men. I wept with wondrous joy.

That night, I also recognized a familiar sound: the intimate expressions I vocalized in my feather-bed prayer closet ... but now magnified by the sounds of children talking to their Father with abandoned love, adoration and respect. The longer I listened, the more I savored the authentic heart cries of faith and absolute trust. Somewhere in the midst of that unforgettable night, that lonely child found the joy of belonging with a bigger expression of family.

I became who they call "The Other Sister."

(Don't get me wrong: my dear parents were vibrant, praying and Bible-studying people. They loved Jesus with all their hearts, and walked with Him in communion and intimacy. But at that time in their lives, it was something to be written about in songs or heralded from a pulpit. True liberated family Bible studies were something we eventually all grew into as our knowledge of Him and His love increased.)

When my sis Jeanne sent me the manuscript for this Easter Bible Study, I was immediately swept back in time to that first of countless Gossett family encounters. It wasn't surprising in the least that she had so perfectly captured on the pages the unique essence of a loving, intelligent, funny, unorthodox, and chocked-full-of-the-Word heart in her passionate pursuit to know Him.

Jeanne is a gifted wordsmith, painting vivid and thought-provoking pictures on her heart canvas. She stretched the mind, and compels you to look again at well-traveled stories of Jesus, to see if perhaps there are secret paths that escaped you in earlier journeys. She is a believer in mysteries and hidden treasures. She might even press you to believe that children are smarter than some give them credit being, and that children deserve to be illuminated by the enlightened mind of Christ.

But she is also forever a barefoot free spirit, in flowing colors, who spends time with her remarkable grandchildren in fields of flowers and butterflies (that's straight out of *"A Bible Fantasy With Jude and Ava"*), singing to her risen King!

Introduction

Contrary to popular (especially secular) opinion, the most important season of the Christian calendar is not Christmas, but Easter. While it is wonderful to enjoy the festivities surrounding the birth of Jesus Christ, there is so much more richness and significance in the last days of His ministry, and the importance of His death and resurrection – yet much of this joy is overlooked.

Many people shiver at the horrible details of Christ's unjust arrest, His brutal beatings, the farcical trials, that humiliating trudge to Golgotha, and finally, His gruesome death. Subsequently, we hesitate to discuss these facts with our children or even among ourselves. Then comes the substitution of twinkly-nosed bunnies, fluffy chicks, curly-coated lambs, colorful eggs, and all kinds of foil-wrapped chocolates – seemingly "benign thieves" taking unlawful precedence over the real story.

Sidebar

Before I go further, let me present this challenge: let us together determine to change the common terminology from "Easter" to "Season of the Lamb."

"Why?" I'm glad you asked! Here is my thought process:

The goddess Ishtar, the light bringer. Babylonian high mother-goddess. Like Inanna, she is the goddess of fertility, love and war. Her cult was the most important one in ancient Babylon, and Ishtar became, under various names, the most important goddess in the Near East and Western Asia.

That's what it says on the "official Ishtar web-site: inanna.virtual.net/ishtar" (if you want to check it out). *"Ishtar"* is also the word from which we Westerners get the word (*gulp!*) *"Easter."*

Uh oh. Many Christians blithely refer to Easter as "the holiest event of the Christian calendar" (as I just did), all the while not realizing we've been duped into acknowledging this ancient Babylonian "goddess" (demon) by this variant of her name! It sort of puts the "Easter Bunny" and all those harmless little eggs and chicks and other "symbols of life renewing, symbols of Spring" into a clearer context, doesn't it? We would be much better sticking to our Judaeo-Christian roots and acknowledge "the Passover" instead of "celebrating Easter."

When I was teaching a Sunday School class of 10-year-olds (which included our grandson Kristian), part of the curriculum was to query the children on their understanding of colored eggs, pretty flowers and cute bunnies. Their answers were very insightful. They all agreed that the secular world isn't going to get excited about "celebrating" the torture and execution of a man ... nor are they likely to buy into the concept of celebrating the "alleged" (yes, one 10-year-old used that word) resurrection of this same convicted criminal. Therefore it is easier for to accept the idea of focusing on bunnies and eggs and other "happy symbols." With the exception of one little girl in our group (of about 30 kids), they all knew of Jesus' death on the cross, and His resurrection, and how the people of His day reacted to all that. Then the children went to Craft Time, making "bumper stickers" with slogans; Kristian's was a drawing of an Easter Bunny with a red circle and a slash across it: *"No Bunnies Allowed."*

We should start a grassroots movement to correctly re-name both Christmas and Easter with more appropriate nomenclature: perhaps **"Christ's Glorious Birth"** and **"Christ's Marvelous Resurrection"** (which could be more familiarly known as "B&R" ... makes you think of ice cream, doesn't it). Believe me, if I could substitute the word *"Easter"* with the phrase **"Season of the Lamb"** as the subtitle of this book, I would – but that makes it tougher for people to figure out what the book is about without that "other designation." Maybe some day it will catch on ....

Past to Present

There are some Bible studies that focus on Theology or Christian History, on variable orthodox or religious opinions and traditions about the

Season of the Lamb. Some present an exhaustive study of why certain denominations begin this season 40 days prior to the main event, yet others downplay it altogether. Mine are Pentecostal roots, and as a child, I recall wearing floaty little dresses with stiff crinolines, complete with fake-flowery hats and tiny gloves (and thinking I was extremely beautiful). I grew up with a series of rather dirge-like songs: *"Were You There When They Crucified My Lord?" ... "The Old Rugged Cross" ... "A Crown of Thorns"* ... and perhaps the most startling: *"Up From the Grave He Arose,"* with its slow, mournful verses and its sprightly chorus.

My mother's mother, Ida Della Shackelford, died on a Lamb's Sunday evening; as a child, I thought it was an appropriate and precious milestone, especially as I gazed at the high-stacked cumulus clouds and imagined Grandma had *"risen up to meet Him in the Air."* Another memory is of a Lamb's Sunday morning sunrise service on a Waikiki beach with dozens of other young "Jesus People," hearing the story of Christ's death and resurrection retold, and then rejoicing as people responded to the salvation call and were baptized in the warm, rolling ocean waves.

Likely because my child-like imagination continues to accompany my child-like faith, throughout this book I have included little fictional vignettes which I hope will enhance the story. **These fictional short stories I have separated with a single asterisk * and a different font.**

Main Point

There **are** positive ways to celebrate the Season of the Lamb. It begins when thoughtful parents give to their children a careful, in-person explanation of all the facts of the death of Jesus. They "lead" their children to the gravesite and "peer" into the quite-empty tomb, generating a new sense of awe, joy and celebration.

The basic fact is this: **Jesus was born to die.** He was always intended to be God's Ultimate Sacrifice, the Lamb of God. Jesus knew this His entire life. Let us together *"behold the Lamb of God Who takes away the sins of the world!"*

Jeanne Halsey
Blaine, Washington
February 2014

Special Instructions For Parents

There are two ways to experience this Bible Study. First is to stretch it out over eight weeks, reading one chapter per week. The second is to blitz it all in Holy Week, with one chapter per day. Either way, here are some suggestions to enhance your studying:

(1) The Bible Reading parts take up a lot of pages, but I've included them here anyway so you don't have to switch back and forth between texts. Have an older child read the provided Bible Reading (or use your own modern-language version of the Bible) out loud; or you can skip the Bible Reading and go straight to the Study. Parents might want to alternate reading the Bible Study, and quizzing the children on the salient points of the Study.

(2) If there are younger children, let them draw pictures of what is being learned while the Bible Study takes place. Their comprehension (or lack thereof) of the Season of the Lamb Story might be better detected by parents through such drawings (and those pictures might eventually become family treasures).

(3) Don't wait until absolutely bed-time to do this Family Bible Study; make it more of a priority, earlier in the day. Also, some of "the devil and his dudes" and crucifixion portions could be frightening to smaller children, probably not the last thing they need to hear before bedtime.

(4) Don't rush through it. Give at least a full hour to this Family Bible Study so you won't be hurried if spontaneous questions-and-answers, discussion, prayer, or personal ministry arise.

(5) If an entire church undertakes this Family Bible Study simultaneously, encourage discussion between other families.

In general, it is important that parents are aware that some of this material may be way over their heads, so you will need to be patient to explain parts they may not understand. Also, there are some details – such as the technically accurate aspects of the crucifixion – that are quite graphic and could be alarming to children; use your best judgement.

As we renew our joy at the incredible sacrifice which the Lamb of God completed for us, I pray that this Season of the Lamb becomes the highest point of the year for you!

Behold the Lamb

Behold the Lamb
Behold the Lamb
Slain from the foundation of the world
For sinners crucified
O holy sacrifice
Behold the Lamb of God
Behold the Lamb

Crown Him, crown Him
Worthy is the Lamb
Praise Him, praise Him
Heaven and Earth resound

Behold the Lamb of God
Behold the Lamb
Slain from the foundation of the world
For sinners crucified
O holy sacrifice
Behold the Lamb of God
Behold the Lamb!

– Dottie Rambo

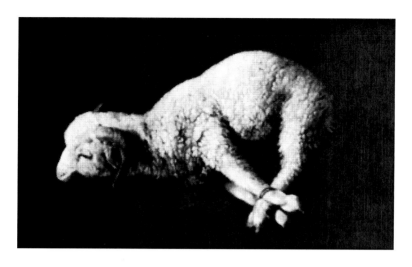

Preface: The Historical Passover Lamb

Passover was the first of three Jewish feast seasons. All Jewish males were required to journey to Jerusalem for a special encounter with and visitation from God. Passover was celebrated during the barley harvest, in the month of Nisan. Instructions for celebrating the feasts are found throughout the Old Testament. Leviticus 23 provides a good summary of them all; Numbers 28 and 29, and Deuteronomy 16 also provide a good summary.

The Passover was to be a memorial to the Hebrews' deliverance from Egypt. This deliverance happened during the month of Nisan and represented God's first encounter with His covenant people. God chose Moses as His instrument to lead the Hebrews out of bondage. Working through Moses, God sent nine terrible plagues against Egypt. This was God's way of convincing Pharaoh to let the Hebrews go. But each time

God sent a new plague, Pharaoh's heart hardened (see Exodus 3 through 10).

God gave Pharaoh every chance to let the Hebrews go, but Pharaoh would not yield. God then declared a tenth and final plague, which was the death of the firstborn of every family (see Exodus 11). But along with this decree of death, God gave specific instructions on how to be saved from the death.

Choosing the Lamb

Every Hebrew man – for our purposes, we'll call him "Matthew" – was to select for his household a lamb without spot or blemish. Matthew was to select this lamb on the tenth day of the month. Then he was to observe this lamb for five days, to make sure there was nothing wrong with him. There could be no fault (spot or blemish) found in this lamb. The lamb lived with the family like a pet – making it even more difficult to slaughter it.

On the fifth day, Matthew was to bring the lamb to his doorstep and slit its throat. As the animal bled out, he would catch the blood in the basin at the foot of the doorstep. Then Matthew would sprinkle the blood on both sides of the door-post and above the door-post. Thus, the entire entrance into the house was covered by the blood of the lamb.

This was to be done in the evening (twilight) of the fourteenth. The Hebrew day begins in the evening at approximately six o'clock. The Hebrews killed the lamb at three o'clock in the afternoon on the fourteenth, in order to eat the meal by six. When three o'clock arrived, they slaughtered the lambs and applied the blood to their door-posts. The family then entered their house through the blood-stained door, where they were protected from the plague of death that was to move through the land.

The Protection of the Blood

According to the instructions, the entire lamb was to be roasted and consumed. Nothing could be left over for the next day. In preparing the meal, not one bone of the lamb was to be broken. To roast a lamb according to these instructions required that the lamb carcass be placed on a spit shaped like a cross-bar, so that its body could be spread open.

Although the family went inside the house and could not see the blood covering, they had faith that God would save them because of it. As they ate their meal, God allowed the Angel of Death to sweep through the land. As he passed from door to door, he sought to enter every household. If the entrance was covered by blood, the Angel of Death could not enter but had to **pass over** that house. The blood was a seal protecting the people inside. However, if the entrance was not covered by blood, judgment would come upon that household and the firstborn would die.

This was the Lord's Passover. And we see that He used the blood of the lamb to save His people from death. The blood of the lamb made atonement for their sins, and was God's way of saving His covenant people.

But the blood of an animal could only **cover** their sins, it could not take them away.

Born to Die

Jesus Christ fulfilled the Feast of Passover in His crucifixion. Since this was the reason for Him being born, Jesus' entire life was pre-destined so that He would fulfill this purpose exactly as God had instructed the Jews to practice it for 1,500 years.

In view of this, as the time approached for Jesus to die, He deliberately arranged His itinerary and personal activities around the events associated with the selection, testing and death of the Passover Lamb (also see the Preface). In this way, the Jewish people would be able to understand Who He was, and what He was doing. Jesus was set aside (to be sacrificed), examined, and crucified on the exact month, day and hour that the Jews had been handling Passover lambs for 1,500 years.

When God established the Passover Feast in Egypt, He instructed the Jews to set aside their lambs on the tenth day of the month of Nisan. In the New Testament we learn that it was the tenth day of the month of Nisan when Jesus entered Jerusalem to be set aside as the Lamb of God (see John 12:1-13). Jesus' triumphal entry into Jerusalem — now usually called Palm Sunday — took place on Sunday, the tenth of Nisan: the exact date that God had told the Jews to set aside their lambs back in Egypt 1,500 years before.

According to Jewish tradition, each family chose its Passover lamb on the tenth day of the month, and carefully examined it until the fourteenth day, to be sure it had no defects. This lamb was to be offered to God. God is perfect; you wouldn't want to offer a lamb to God that was blemished. So the Jews observed and tested the lamb for five days to make sure it was faultless, not only in outward appearance but also in inward character.

During His last week of public ministry, God's own Lamb (see John 1:29) was examined in various ways for five days, and He passed every test. He often understood the questions better than those asking them, and He responded with wisdom and honesty.

The motives of people asking Jesus these various questions were also varied: some deliberately tried to trick Him (see Mark 12:13); some genuinely searched for truth (v. 37); some responded to His miraculous signs and wonders; others tested His knowledge of God's laws (vv. 24, 28, 32, 34).

What motivated people to "investigate" Jesus in our day? Many grow up with Judaeo-Christian concepts taught to them, but Jesus doesn't become real to them until later years. Others come from a sin-filled life, and are attracted to the purity and love of Jesus. Still others turn to Him in desperation, at the end of their rope, and find peace, forgiveness, cleansing readily available to them. Some take the intellectual approach to the reality of Jesus Christ ... and like Nicodemus (see John 3:1-21, 18-27), they find His answers to the hard issues of life acceptable.

Jesus At the Passover Supper

As Jesus and His disciples ate the traditional Passover Supper of roast lamb, unleavened bread, bitter herbs, and wine (see Exodus 12:8), He taught them many things (and the four Gospels each detail that night distinctly differently). But the common theme He carefully explained to men (who still did not grasp it): *"I AM the Lamb of God, and I have willingly come to offer Myself as a Sacrifice for all men. I have come to die."*

How else could He tear a loaf of bread apart and offer it to His disciples, saying, *"Take, eat, this is My Body, broken for you. Do this in remembrance of Me"* (Mark 14:22; also see I Corinthians 11:25) – unless His physical body was about to be torn apart by executioners?

How else could He pour out the wine and pass the cup around, saying, *"Take, drink, this is My*

Blood of the New Covenant, which is shed for many. Do this in remembrance of Me" (Mark 14:23-24; also see I Corinthians 11:25-26) – unless His life's blood was about to stream out of His body through wounds on His back, His head, His hands and feet, His chest and side?

How else could they begin to **remember** Him – unless He died and went away from them?

Jesus was the perfect Lamb (see I Peter 1:18-19) Who **had to die** to save us. We are saved, not by admiring His example or by studying His teachings, but by believing He IS the Son of God, by applying His Blood to our own hearts by faith.

The lamb saved the Hebrews in Egypt, and it sustained them for their journey. We "feed" on Jesus Christ when we meditate on His Word, making it a part of our inner persons.

An Historical Footnote

Josephus, a first-century Jewish historian, reported that there were about 256,500 lambs killed in Jerusalem the year Jesus was crucified. With this many lambs, it was necessary for the Jews to prepare them for sacrifice at nine o'clock in the morning of the fourteenth day of Nisan. Then they killed them at three o'clock that after-noon, so that the Passover meal could be com-pleted before six o'clock, which would begin a new day.

At the **exact hour** when the Jews were preparing their lambs for sacrifice, Jesus was nailed to the cross. Mark wrote, *"Now it was the third hour, and they crucified Him"* (15:25). The third hour was nine o'clock in the morning Jewish time.

Passover Fulfilled

In fulfillment of the Feast of Passover and Isaiah's prophecy, Jesus bore our griefs and carried our sorrows. He was wounded for our transgressions and bruised for our iniquities. The Lord God laid on Jesus the iniquity of us all. He was oppressed and afflicted. Yet He opened not His mouth, like a lamb led to the slaughter.

At three o'clock, as the people were praising God and slaughtering their Passover lambs, Jesus died. Mark was careful to note the time and wrote that it was the ninth hour (three o'clock Jewish time) when Jesus breathed His last breath (see 15:33-37).

Jesus gave His total self to be roasted and consumed in the judgment fires of God as He died for our sins. The spit on which the Passover lamb were spread open was shaped like a cross-bar – which foreshadowed Jesus hanging on the cross of Calvary.

All the other details concerning the death of the Passover lamb happened to Jesus, the real Lamb of God, exactly. For example, His bones were not broken. Remember that God had said not to break any bones in the Passover lambs (see Exodus 12:46; Numbers 9:12; Psalm 34:20)? When a person is crucified, his body sags so that he cannot breathe. This causes him to push himself up with his heels just long enough to take a deep breath. To hasten the person's death, a Roman soldier would break his legs; thus he would not be able to push himself up to get air, but would suffocate.

John records that the soldiers routinely broke the legs of the two thieves who were crucified on either side of Jesus. But when they came to Jesus, they saw that He was already dead and did not break His legs (see John 19:31-33). When John realized this, he wrote: *"For these things were done that the Scripture should be fulfilled: 'Not one of His bones shall be broken'"* (John 19:36; also see Psalm 34:20).

Day 1 (Palm Sunday):
A Lamb On a Colt

BIBLE READING

The Triumphal Entry

As they were approaching Jerusalem and came to Bethphage and Bethany at the Mount of Olives, Jesus sent two of His disciples, saying, "Go to the village ahead of you, and just as you enter it, you will find a colt tied there, which no one has ever ridden. Untie it and bring it here. If anyone asks you, 'Why are you doing this?', tell him, 'The Lord needs it, and will send it back shortly'."

They went and found a colt outside in the street, tied at a doorway. As they untied it, some people standing there asked, "What are you doing, untying that colt?" They answered as Jesus had told them to, and the people let them go.

When they brought the colt to Jesus and threw their cloaks over it, He sat on it. Many people spread their cloaks on the road, while others spread branches they had cut in the fields. Those who went ahead and those who followed shouted, "Hosanna! Blessed is He Who comes in the Name of the Lord! Blessed is the coming kingdom of our father David! Hosanna in the highest."

Jesus entered Jerusalem and went to the Temple. He looked around at everything, but since it was already late, He went out to Bethany with the Twelve.

The Fig Tree is Cursed

The next day as they were leaving Bethany, Jesus was hungry. Seeing in the distance a fig tree in leaf, He went to find out if it had any fruit. When He reached it, He found nothing but leaves, because it was not the season for figs. Then He said to the tree, "May no one ever eat fruit from you again!" And His disciples heard Him say it.

The Temple is Cleansed

On reaching Jerusalem, Jesus entered the Temple area and began driving out those who were buying and selling there. He overturned the tables of the money-changers and the benches of those selling doves,and would not allow anyone to carry merchandise through the Temple courts. And as He taught them, He said, "Is it not written: 'My House will be called a House of Prayer for all nations'? But you have made it a den of robbers!" The chief priests and the teachers of the Law heard this and began looking for a way to kill Him, for they feared Him because the whole crowd was amazed at His teaching.

The Power of Faith

When evening came, they went out of the city. In the morning as they went along, they saw the fig tree withered from the roots. Peter remembered and said to Jesus, "Rabbi, look: the fig tree You cursed has withered!"

"Have faith in God," Jesus answered. "I tell you the truth: if anyone says to this mountain, 'Go throw yourself into the sea,' and does not doubt in his heart but believes that what he says will happen, it will be done for him. Therefore I tell you, whatever you ask for in prayer, believe that you have received it, and it will be yours. And when you stand praying, if you hold anything against anyone, forgive him, so that your Father in Heaven may forgive you your sins."

Mark 11:1-26; paraphrased

ഏ

BIBLE STUDY

Imagine this picture: a fluffy little white lamb, calmly perched on the back of a colt, which is trotting into town in the center of a noisy crowd of people! When Jesus rode the unbroken colt into Jerusalem, He was fulfilling thousands of years of prophecies (see 1 Kings 1:32-40, Zechariah 9:9), for He was indeed that innocent Lamb of God – while also the Mighty Prince of Peace.

"Hosanna! Blessed is He Who comes in the Name of the Lord! Blessed is the kingdom of our father David, Who comes in

the Name of the Lord! Hosanna in the
highest!"

Mark 11:9-10

Does that *"Hosanna in the highest"* part remind
you of any other time in Jesus life? Like when a
sky-wide choir of angels sang that same refrain
(see Luke 2:13-15)?

About the Colt

For three years, Jesus has been working as an
itinerant preacher, and His teachings and miracles
had become widespread knowledge, popular with
the common people – but threatening to religious
leaders (Pharisees). Therefore, when the disciples
asked some villagers at Bethphage (Mark 11:1-6)
to freely give up their valuable colt, is it likely these
generous people were also the "seeds" of an early
"underground church"?

That colt was a precious asset to those
villagers. It represented livelihood and value. Yet
they gave it freely for the Master's use. Today it
seems harder to hear the voice of God asking us
to give up certain "valuables" for His sake – such
as taking "our valuable time" to tell someone the
Good News, or sublimating our "valuable rights" in
order to be kind or thoughtful to someone else, or
stopping to pray with a person in need or maybe
just to listen to them.

The Bible specifically says the colt was
"unbroken," had never before been ridden. Can

you picture Jesus dressed as a cowboy at a rodeo, swaggering up to a skittish colt and riding it "bucking bronco" style? No, I can't either. I believe the colt recognized the Son of God, and willingly submitted to Him. The colt must have felt very secure in the company of Jesus because the noise of the welcoming crowd was thunderous!

The Underground Church

Further evidence of this "underground church" movement is found in Mark 14:13-16, where a "secret sign" was passed by the disciples to a follower of Jesus when they were preparing for the Passover Super. It was not typically the task of men to fetch water; it was a job usually assigned to women (or slaves). Therefore, when a man was assigned to be the water-carrier, that likely meant plans for the Upper Room were prearranged, part of elaborate "security measures" or precautions. Later, when the frightened disciples went into hiding after Jesus' execution, they found refuge with these same supportive people, whose residence included the "upper room."

The Triumphal Entry

When Jesus rode into Jerusalem, the common people welcomed Him with loud enthusiasm, joyously proclaiming Him as King. However, their behavior was very unpopular with the religious leaders, who protested to Jesus, *"Teacher, tell Your disciples to be quiet!"* (Luke 19:39; paraphrased).

His answer – appropriate for that day **and** this – was such a classic:

"If these (rejoicing people) should keep silent, then the rocks and stones would immediately cry out!"
Luke 19:40 (also see **Habakkuk 2:12**)

There is another time when "the Establishment" disapproved of a raucous scene of rejoicing believers, an event which took place (coincidentally?) in the streets of Jerusalem:

So David, and the elders of Israel, and the commanders of units of a thousand, went to bring up the Ark of the Covenant of the Lord from the house of Obed-Edom, with rejoicing. ... Now David was clothed in a robe of fine linen, as were all the Levites who were carrying the Ark, and as were the musicians, and Kenaniah, who was in charge of the singing of the choirs. David also wore a linen ephod. So all Israel brought up the Ark of the Covenant of the Lord with shouts, with the sounding of rams' horns and trumpets, and of cymbals, and the playing of lyres and harps. As the Ark of the Covenant of the Lord was entering the City of David, Michel, daughter of Saul, watched from a window. And when she saw King David dancing and celebrating, she despised him in her heart.
1 Chronicles 15:25, 27-29

To recap quickly: Michel was the daughter of King Saul, and David's first wife; she represented the previous royal family. Separated from David during his years of exile which were caused by her maniac (possibly bipolar) father, Michel was forcibly divorced from him, remarried to another; during those exile years, David married several other women. Then when David became king after Saul's death, Michel was forcibly divorced from her second husband (whom she had learned to love) and returned to David – his "trophy wife." She was not a happy woman, and she criticized David for his "unseemly" behavior. Centuries later, when Jesus – the Son descended from the House of David – entered Jerusalem in a crowd of cheering, happy people, the Pharisees (the "old guard") looked on the scene with a very similar disdain.

Praise is such a necessary part of our relationship with God! No one (least of all God) ever said that we had to be quiet, soft-spoken, mild-mannered in our praise to God – that can be alright, but it is not the only way. It is our privilege to sing, to shout, to dance, to wave our hands (or palm branches), to get all excited about Who God is today! I am certain that if Jesus came riding into town in a Corvette convertible, He would receive a joyous, unrestrained welcome – maybe even a ticker-tape parade – from His people today.

Much to Learn From the Unfortunate Fig Tree

Jesus' experience with the fig tree (Mark 11:12-14, 20-26) was further evidence that He was indeed related to the Creator. By His Word, all things were created (see Psalm 148:5) ... and by His Word, that fig tree was cursed forever. Similarly, the fig tree symbolizes plants which take up space but produce no fruit – certainly not the kind of people we want to be!

"What kind of fruit are people supposed to produce? We are humans, not plants!" Great question! God is looking for people who are willing to live His way, who have personality characteristics that please Him. Dr. Eugene Peterson explains it this way:

> *But what happens when we live God's way? He brings gifts into our lives, much the same way that fruit appears in an orchard – things like affection for others, exuberance about life, serenity. We develop a willingness to stick with things, a sense of compassion in the heart, and a conviction that a basic holiness permeates things and people. We find ourselves involved in loyal commitments, not needing to force our way in life, able to marshal and direct our energies wisely.*
> **Galatians 5:22-23; the Message**

When a person chooses to emulate (being like Jesus) his Heavenly Father, this "good fruit" shows up in many areas of life. Matthew 3:10 describes the fate of unfruitful trees (and unfruitful disciples):

> *Every tree that does not bear good fruit is cut down at the roots and thrown into the fire.*
>
> **Matthew 3:10; NAS**

You may ask: *"But why did Jesus curse the fig tree for not bearing fruit **before** the season? The Bible says it was full of leaves, but it was too early for bearing fruit too. Wasn't that unfair? And how does all this relate to people today?"*

More good questions ... and the answers are a bit complicated. I asked a horticulturalist this question, and his reply was, *"There are many instances when a horticulturalist will look at a long row of nearly-identical trees, walking up and down the rows, and training their eyes learn to spot which plants are going to be good fruit-bearers, and which ones will have puny little fruit or, more likely, no fruit at all. This means those trees have not engaged in the process of replication; something has gone wrong internally and no amount of fertilizing or pruning or setting into the most propitious soil with ample sunlight and watering – these are not going to change the nature of the tree. As cross-pollinators, they are neither male nor female in their attributes; they are, essentially, eunuchs. Ultimately, those unfruitful trees are thrown out because they are wasting valuable ground space and supplements, which could be devoted to another tree."*

"Eunuchs?" Could this also refer to Christians who sit happily in the pew – enjoying all the benefits of being a Christian – but who do not demonstrate the *"fruit of the Spirit"*? How about those who have no intention of also becoming a soul-winners, of spiritually reproducing and discipling others?

> *"I am the True Vine, and My Father is the Gardener. He cuts off every branch in Me that bears no fruit; while every branch that does bear fruit, He prunes so that it will be even more fruitful. ... I am the Vine, and you are the branches. If you remain in Me and I in you, you will bear much fruit; apart from Me you can do nothing. If you do not remain in Me, you are like a branch that is thrown away and withers; such branches are picked up, thrown into the fire and burned.*
>
> **John 15:1-2, 5-6**

God **does** hold us accountable for the **condition** of our hearts, and He **does** expect us to "bear good fruit." If Christian believers fail to demonstrate the fruit of the Spirit, then He has a remedy: He puts us in the fire. Now before you think that this is the same as burning completely, total destruction, remember that we are **all** tried in the "fires of God":

> *Praise our God, all people, let the sound of His praise be heard; he has preserved our lives and kept our feet from slipping. For*

You, God, tested us; **You refined us [in the fire] like silver.** *You brought us into prison and laid burdens on our backs. You let people ride over our heads;* **we went through fire** *and water, but* **You brought us to a place of abundance.**

Psalm 66:8-12; emphasis added

In all this you greatly rejoice, though now for a little while you may have had to suffer grief in all kinds of trials. These have come so that the proven genuineness of your faith – of greater worth than gold, which perishes even though **refined by fire** *– may result in praise, glory and honor when Jesus Christ is revealed.*

1 Peter 1:6-7; emphasis added

Throughout our lifetimes, God continues to work in our hearts, constantly refining our natures so that we exhibit the fruit of the Spirit in everything we say and do. Let this be a warning to non-fruitful Christians who are happy with holding their "ticket to Heaven" but who don't care about continuing to obey God's command to *"be fruitful and multiply"* (meaning "sharing the love of Christ and showing others the way of salvation").

The Truth About the Temple Cleansing

People traveled great distances to come to Jerusalem for the Passover; they could not easily carry a sacrificial lamb, goat or dove with them. Therefore the chief priests permitted merchants to sell animals and birds for sacrifice within the Temple courts. But greed and corruption crept into the hearts of the merchants and money-changers because they began to prey on the travelers by charging exorbitant prices for inferior sacrifices, and using imbalanced scales when measuring coins. These was evidence of spiritual unfruitfulness.

Before Jesus arrived in Jerusalem, He knew He would encounter a mess in the Temple courts. Those who were allegedly representing God (the priesthood) were portraying God the Father as mean and unjust. Jesus came to war with the kingdom of darkness, restoring the Name, the character, the integrity of His Father:

For our struggle is not against flesh and blood, but against the rulers, against the authorities, against the powers of this dark world, and against the spiritual forces of evil in the heavenly realms.
Ephesians 6:12

The entire episode of "cleansing of the Temple" was not a burst of anger but was a very calculated action.   His desire was not punishment – His whole purpose in coming to Earth was to exhibit God's eternal love:

God did not send His Son into the world to condemn the world, but to save the world through Him.
John 3:17

Similarly, His treatment of the fig tree was not because He was having a hunger attack, but because He was demonstrating to the disciples what He would do about unfruitfulness, whether in vegetables or humans ... and that He came to make a Godly "course correction."

There are many instances in the Gospels where Jesus' actions or words "foretold" the future, immediate or distant. He was not a man meandering His way through Israel, taking His time to gather a bunch of followers – He knew his time was limited to impact the whole world with His human life before He ultimately laid down that life as the final sacrifice; He knew He was the Lamb of God ... and He didn't have time to waste on unfruitful anything. He packed a **lot** into those three years of ministry!

Why would the religious leaders object to Jesus cleansing the Temple of merchants and commerce? In addition to misrepresenting the nature of God, was it because they were profiting from the greed-infested sales of sacrificial animals and birds? Were they also taking a cut from the money-changers' profits? It had happened before: in the days of Eli the prophet, his own sons were guilty of selling sacrificial meat for personal gain (see 1 Samuel 2:12-17) and other abominations.

Jesus' apparently harsh response against a plush but fruit-less tree was not a temper tantrum. He was demonstrating God's own attitude toward people who like to look good on the outside but who have cold hearts (see Isaiah 64:6). Let us endeavor to not just uselessly or selfishly take up space in God's Garden but to become fruit-bearing (Spirit-defined, Christ-reproducing) trees!

Jesus and the Bad Guys

In Mark 11:15-18, it appears Jesus was under some degree of stress because His strong reaction to the Temple money-changers was quite unlike the gentle Teacher from Nazareth. He was, however, fully justified in driving out unholiness from His Father's all-holy House. Psalm 93:5 says, *"Holiness adorns Your House, O God."* The leaders were not "praying" – they were **preying** on the people, using "religion" to make money.

We sometimes glide right over Mark 11:11, but it is significant to understand Jesus' actions during this time:

> *Jesus entered Jerusalem and went into the Temple courts. He looked around at everything, but since it was already late, He went out to Bethany with the Twelve.*
> **Mark 11:11**

What Jesus was about to do in the Temple on the very next day was not the result of a sudden fit of anger. Jesus had already been to the Temple and had clearly seen the money-changers and merchandisers at work. His fury had all night to simmer ... and it *is* possible He vented **some** of that righteous anger on that "seemingly innocent" fig tree.

The strain He was undergoing had nothing to do with His impending physical death. From the moment He walked up to God's Throne in Heaven and asked for the privilege of redeeming Mankind from the eternal curse of sin, Jesus was earmarked for sacrificial death, He was **willingly** the Lamb of God. It is my belief that Jesus was already anticipating the critical moment when He would be cut off from the ever-flowing current of fellowship He enjoyed with His Heavenly Father. Jesus had always been in contact with God.

That fellowship of Father to Son, of Spirit to Spirit, was one Jesus depended on for direction, sustenance, guidance, strength, wisdom, power – His very life! This soon-coming break in fellowship (when Jesus would take upon Himself **all** the sin of Mankind forever ... and we know that God cannot abide sin at all) was one He would have preferred to avoid:

> *"Father, take this cup (trial, ordeal, frightening experience) away from Me. Nevertheless, not what I prefer, but what You require."*
>
> **Mark 14:36;** paraphrased

We too seek to fellowship with the Father on a constant basis:

So the Church ... enjoyed peace, being built up and walking in the fear of the Lord and in the comfort of the Holy Spirit, continuing to increase (being fruitful).
Acts 9:31

If we live by the Spirit, let us also walk by the Spirit.
Galatians 5:25

When we fellowship with our Heavenly Father on a continual, daily basis, then we too receive an unbroken current of direction, sustenance, guidance, strength, wisdom, power – His very life becomes ours!

Prerequisites for Effective Prayer

In Mark 11:22-26, we learn important truths about the value of prayer, and right ways to pray. **Prayer must always be mixed with faith ... and prayer must always be preceded by forgiveness.**

Effective communication with the Father (generally known as "prayer") is so important that Jesus continually instructed us on this subject. In Luke 18, He detailed various types of prayer: confident prayer (verses 1-8) ... arrogant prayer (verses 9-17) ... ignorant prayer (verses 18-27) ... persistent prayer (verses 35;-43).

In Luke 17, He described faith and its various characteristics: faith to forgive (verses 1-4) ... faith to serve (verses 5-10) ... faith to pray (verses 11-19) ... faith to be ready when He comes (verses 20-37).

Before prayer mixed with faith can be effective, there must always be repentance (recognizing your wayward), forgiveness (making things right) and restoration (walking in wholeness):

> *"If you bring your (prayer) to the altar and there remember that your brother has something against you, leave your gift there before the altar and go your way to be reconciled with your brother; then return and offer your gift."*
>
> **Matthew 5:23-24**

> *"Be merciful, just as your Father is merciful. Judge not, and you shall not be judged; condemn not, and you shall not be condemned; forgive, and you will be forgiven."*
>
> **Luke 6:36-37**

> *Let all bitterness, wrath, anger, clamor, evil-speaking, and malice be put away from you. Be kind to one another, tender-hearted, forgiving one another, even as God in Christ forgave you.*
>
> **Ephesians 4:32**

Repentance ... **forgiveness** ... **restoration** –
these are necessary steps to make our prayers
effective.

One More Thing

Jesus Christ fulfilled the Feast of the Passover
in His crucifixion. Since this was the whole reason
for Him being born into humanity, Jesus' entire life
was predestined so that He would fulfill this purpose exactly as God had instructed the Jews to
practice it for 1,500 years.

In view of this, as the time approached for
Jesus to die, He deliberately arranged His itinerary
and personal activities around the events associated with the selection, testing and death of the
Passover lamb (also see the Preface). In this way,
the Jewish people – and all Mankind – would be
able to understand Who He was and what He was
doing. Jesus was set aside (to be sacrificed),
examined and then crucified on the exact month,
day and hour that the Jews had been handling
Passover lambs for 1,500 years.

When God established the Passover Feast in
Egypt, He instructed the Jews to set aside their
lambs on the tenth day of the month of Nisan. In
the New Testament we learn that it was the tenth
day of the month of Nisan when Jesus entered
Jerusalem on the back of the untried colt to be set
aside as the Lamb of God (see John 12:1-13).
Jesus' triumphal entry into Jerusalem – now
usually called "Palm Sunday" – took place on
Sunday, the tenth of Nisan: the exact date God

had told the Jews to set aside their lambs, way back in Egypt 1,500 years before! Coincidence? Not at all!

ഏൗ

BIBLE QUIZ

(1.a) What did the people of Jerusalem say when Jesus entered the city riding on a colt?

"Hosanna in the highest! Blessed be the King Who comes in the Name of the Lord!" (see Mark 11:9-10)

(1.b) When were those words heard before?

When the angels sang about Jesus on the day He was born. (see Luke 2:13-15)

(2) What happens when we begin to live God's way?

We begin to produce spiritual fruit, such as: love, joy, peace, patience, kindness, goodness, faithfulness, gentleness, self-control. (see Galatians 5:22-23)

(3) What are some prerequisites for effective prayer?

First, forgiveness, repentance, restoration; then faith. ["Before prayer mixed with faith can be effective, there must always be repentance (acknowledging sin, turning away from it towards God), forgiveness (making things right with others) and restoration (walking in wholeness)."]

Day 2 (Monday):
"Who Is This Man, Anyway?"

BIBLE READING

A Question of Authority

Jesus and His disciples arrived again in Jerusalem, and while He was walking in the Temple courts, the chief priests, the teachers of the Law and the elders came to Him. "By what authority are You doing these things?" they asked. "And who gave You authority to do this?"

Jesus replied, "I will ask you question; answer Me, and I will tell you by what authority I am doing these things. John's baptism: was it from Heaven or from men? Tell Me!"

They discussed it among themselves, "If we say, 'From Heaven,' He will ask, 'Then why didn't you believe him?' But if we say, 'From men ...'" (for they feared the people, for everyone held that John really was a prophet). So they finally answered Jesus, "We don't know."

Jesus said, "Neither will I tell you by what authority I AM doing these things."

Jesus Rebukes Them Through Parables

He then began to speak to them in parables: "A man planted a vineyard. He put a wall around it, dug a pit for the wine-press and built a watchtower. Then he rented the vineyard to some farmers and went away on a journey.

"At harvest time, he sent a servant to the tenants to collect from them some of the fruit of the vineyard. But they seized the servant, beat him and sent him away empty-handed. Then he sent another servant to them; they struck this man on the head and treated him shamefully. He sent still another, and that one they killed. He sent many others; some of them they beat, others they killed.

"He had one left to send, a son, whom he loved. He sent him last of all, saying, 'They will respect my son.'

"But the tenants said to one another, 'This is the heir. Come, let's kill him, and the inheritance will be ours.' So they took him and killed him, and threw him out of the vineyard.

"What then will the owner of the vineyard do? He will come and kill all those tenants, and give the vineyard to others! Haven't you read this Scripture: 'The stone the builders rejected has become the capstone; the Lord has done this, and it is marvelous in our eyes'?" (see Psalm 118:22)

Then they looked for a way to arrest Him because they knew He had spoken the parable against them. But they were afraid of the crowd, so they left Him and went away.

They Try to Trick Him

Later they sent some of the Pharisees and Herodians to Jesus, to catch Him in His words. They came to Him and said, "Teacher, we know You are a Man of integrity. You aren't swayed by men because You pay no attention to who they are; but You teach the way of God in accordance with the truth. Is it right to pay taxes to Caesar or not? Should we pay or shouldn't we?"

But Jesus knew their hypocrisy. "Why are you trying to trap Me?" He asked. "Bring Me a denarius and let Me look at it." They brought the coin, and He asked them, "Whose portrait is this, and whose inscription?"

"Caesar's," they replied.

Then Jesus said to them, "Give to Caesar what is Caesar's and to God what is God's." And they were amazed at Him.

Then the Sadducees (who say there is no resurrection) came to Him with a question. "Teacher," they said, "Moses wrote for us that if a man's brother dies and leaves a wife but no children, the man must marry the widow and have children for his brother.

"Now there are seven brothers. The first one married and died without leaving any children. The second one married the widow, but he also died, leaving no child. It was the same with the third. In fact, none of the seven left any children. Last of all, the woman died too. At the resurrection, whose wife will she be, since all seven were married to her?"

Jesus replied, "Are you not in error because you do not know the Scriptures or the power of God? When the dead rise, they will neither marry nor be given in marriage; they will be like the angels in Heaven. Now about the dead rising – have you not read in the Book of Moses, in the account of the bush, how God said to him, 'I AM the God of Abraham, the God of Isaac and the God of Jacob' (see Exodus 3:6)? He is not the God of the dead, but of the living. You are badly mistaken!"

Some Leaders Respond Favorably

One of the teachers of the Law came and heard them debating. Noticing that Jesus had given them a good answer, he asked Him, "Of all the commandments, which is the most important?"

"The most important one," answered Jesus, "is this: 'Hear O Israel, the Lord our God, the Lord is One. Love the Lord your God with all your heart, with all your soul, with all your mind, and with all your strength.' The second is this: 'Love your neighbor as yourself.' There is no commandment greater than these."

"Well said, Teacher," the man replied. "You are right in saying that God is One and there is no other but Him. To love Him with all your heart, with all your understanding and with all your strength, and to love your neighbor as yourself is more important than all burnt offerings and sacrifices."

When Jesus saw that he had answered wisely, He said to him, "You are not far from the Kingdom of God." And from then on, no one dared to ask Him any more questions.

While Jesus was teaching in the Temple courts, He asked, "How is it that the teachers of the Law say that the Christ is the son of David? David himself, speaking by the Holy Spirit, declared: 'The Lord said to my Lord, "Sit at My right hand until I put Your enemies under Your feet" (see Psalm 110:1).'

"David himself calls Him 'Lord.' How then can he be His son?" The large crowd listened to Him with delight.

Jesus Warns the Common People

As He taught, Jesus said, "Watch out for the teachers of the Law. They like to walk around in flowing robes and be greeted in the marketplaces, and have the most important seats in the synagogue and the places of honor at banquets. They devour widows' houses, and for a show make lengthy prayers. Such men will be punished most severely."

Jesus sat down opposite the place where the offerings were put, and watched the crowd putting their money into the Temple Treasury. Many rich people threw in large amounts. But a poor widow came and put in two very small copper coins, worth only a fraction of a penny. Calling His disciples to Him, Jesus said, "I tell you the truth, this poor widow has put more into the Treasury than all the others. They all gave out of their wealth, but she gave out of her poverty, put in everything, all she had to live on."

Prophecies About the Last Days

As He was leaving the Temple, one of His disciples said to Him, "Look, Teacher! What massive stones! What magnificent buildings!"

"Do you see all these great buildings?" replied Jesus. "Not one stone here will be left on another; every one will be thrown down."

As Jesus was sitting on the Mount of Olives opposite the Temple, Peter, James, John, and Andrew asked Him privately, "Tell us, when will these things happen? And what will be the sign that they are all about to to fulfilled?"

Jesus said to them, "Watch out that no one deceives you. Many will come in My Name, claiming, 'I am He,' and will deceive many. When you hear of wars and rumors of wars, do not be alarmed. Such things must happen, but the end is still to come. Nation will rise against nation, and kingdom against kingdom. There will be earthquakes in various places, and famines. These are the beginning of birth pains.

"Be On Guard!"

"You must be on your guard. You will be handed over to the local councils and flogged in the synagogues. On account of Me, you will stand before governors and kings as witnesses to them. And the Gospel must first be preached to all nations. Whenever you are arrested and brought to trial, do not worry beforehand about what to say. Just say whatever is given you at the time, for it is not you speaking but the Holy Spirit.

"Brother will betray brother to death, and a father his child. Children will rebel against their parents and have them put to death. All men will hate you because of Me, but he who stands firm to the end will be saved.

"When you see the abomination that causes desolation standing where it does not belong – let the reader understand – then let those who are in Judea flee to the mountains. Let no one on the roof of his house go down or enter the house to take anything out. Let no one in the field go back to get his cloak. How dreadful it will be in those days for pregnant women and nursing mothers! Pray that this will not take place in winter, because those will be days of distress unequaled from the beginning, when God created the world, until now – and never to be equaled again.

Beware of False Messiahs

"If the Lord had not cut short those days, no one would survive. But for the sake of the elect, when He has chosen, He has shortened them. At that time, if anyone says to you, 'Look, here is the Christ!' or 'Look, there He is!' – do not believe it! For false Christs and false prophets will appear and perform signs and miracles to deceive the elect – if that were possible. So be on your guard; I have told you everything ahead of time.

"But in those days following that distress, the sun will be darkened and the moon will not give its light; the stars will fall *from the sky, and the heavenly bodies will be shaken (see Isaiah 13:10, 34:4). At that time, men will see the Son of Man coming in clouds, with great power and glory. And He will send His angels and gather His elect from the four winds, from the ends of the Earth to the ends of the Heavens.*

"Now learn this lesson from the fig tree: As soon as its twigs get tender and its leaves come out, you know that summer is near. Even so, when you see these things happening, you know that it is near, right at your door.

"I tell you this truth: This generation will certainly not pass away until all these things have happened. Heaven and Earth will pass away, but My Words will never pass away. No on knows that day or hour, not even the angels in Heaven, nor the Son, but only the Father. Be on guard! Be alert! You do not know when that time will come.

"It's like a man going away. He leaves His house in the charge of his servants, each with his assigned task, and tells the one at the door to keep watch. Therefore keep watch because you do not know when the owner of the house will come back – whether in the evening or at midnight, or when the rooster crows or at dawn. If he comes suddenly, do not let him find you sleeping. What I say to you, I say to everyone: Watch!"

Mark 11:26-33, 12:44, 13:1-37; paraphrased

BIBLE STUDY

"Who is Jesus of Nazareth?" This question was uppermost in the minds of the religious leaders of the day. There were very disturbed by His teachings; they were unsuccessful in tripping up His doctrine; they feared His power and author-ity greatly. They never, ever recognized His true identity: the beloved, only-begotten Son of God Almighty Himself, now willingly laying down His life as the ultimate Lamb of God ... ready to die for them.

Death did not catch Jesus by surprise. From the moment He stepped up to His Father's Throne in Heaven and asked to be allowed to become the Ultimate Sacrifice on Earth, He knew He was sentenced to die. The Old Covenant (Old Testa-ment) sacrifice of a lamb was God's original way to dispel the effects of sin (see Leviticus 4:27-31; also Hebrews 10:1-14), the shedding of blood was His method of removing the stain of transgression. And Jesus **volunteered** to leave His Heavenly Home, go to sin-filled Earth, be born as a helpless Baby, grow up incognito among men, and – eventually – give up His life by one of the cruelest forms of execution ever devised.

Some Truly Recognized Him

His Mother knew Who He was. Mary had heard the message of the angel, who plainly told her she would give birth to the divine Son of God:

"You will conceive in your womb and bring forth a Son, and shall call His Name Jesus. He will be great, and will be called the Son of the Highest; and the Lord God will give Him the Throne of His Father, David. And He will reign over the House of Jacob forever, and of His Kingdom there will be no end."

Luke 1:30-33

Later, when Mary and Joseph brought Baby Jesus to the Temple in Jerusalem, two inspired prophets, Simeon and Anna, met them and acknowledged the birth of the Messiah. Simeon said to Mary:

"Behold,this Child is destined for the fall and rising of many in Israel, and for a sign which will be spoken against, that the thoughts of many hearts may be revealed. A sword will pierce through your own soul also."

Luke 2:34-35

As a Child of twelve years, Jesus reminded His earthly parents of Who He really was:

Jesus said to Joseph and Mary, "Why do you see Me? Did you not know that I must be about My Father's business?"

Luke 2:49

Mary also knew what Jesus' mission was, and what He was capable of doing. In John 2:1-11, she asked Him to perform a miracle at a wedding. At first, He was reluctant to reveal His supernatural powers publicly – and because He knew that once His powers were revealed, the clock started ticking on the countdown to Calvary – but His compassion compelled Him to help people in their time of need.

His cousin knew Who He was. When John the Baptist, prophesying and baptizing sinners out in the wilderness, saw his Cousin Jesus approaching, he openly recognized Him as the Messiah (a fact which he had personally known since **before** his own birth; see Luke 1:41-45). John proclaimed:

> *"Behold the Lamb of God, Who takes away the sin of the world! ... I have seen and testified that He is the Son of God."*
> **John 1:32, 34**

When John the Baptist was executed by King Herod, Jesus mourned His cousin's death (see Matthew 14:13), for He had lost one of the few who actually recognized His true identity.

Choosing a Lamb

According to Jewish tradition, each family chose its Passover lamb on the tenth day of the month, and carefully examined it until the fourteenth day, to be sure it had no defects. This lamb was to be offered to God. God is perfect – you wouldn't offer a lamb to God that was blemished.

So the Jews observed and tested the lamb for five days to make sure it was faultless, not only in outward appearance but also in inward character.

During His last week of public ministry, God's own Lamb (see John 1:29) was examined in various ways for five days, and He passed every test. He often understood the questions better than those asking them, and He responded with wisdom and honesty.

The motives of the people asking Jesus these various questions were also varied: some deliberately tried to trick Him (Mark 12:13) ... some genuinely searched for truth (verse 37) ... some responded to His miraculous signs and wonders ... others tested His knowledge of God's Laws (verses 24, 28, 32, 34).

What motivates people to "investigate" Jesus in our day? Many grow up with Judaeo-Christian concepts taught to them, but Jesus doesn't become real to them until later years. Others come from a sin-filled life, and are attracted to the purity and love of Jesus. Still others turn to Him in desperation, at the ends of their rope, and find peace, forgiveness, cleansing readily available to them. Some take the intellectual approach to the reality of Jesus Christ ... and like Nicodemus (see John 3:1-21, 18-27), they find His answers to the hard issues of life acceptable.

What Was So Controversial About Jesus?

Among the important things Jesus taught during His last week was:

"You shall love the Lord your God with all your heart, with all your soul, with all your mind, and with all your strength. This is the first commandment.

"And the second like it is: You shall love your neighbor as yourself. There is no other commandment greater than these."
Mark 12:30-31

What was so controversial that Jesus taught about love? Because Jesus could see into the hearts of men (see 1 Samuel 16:7), He knew they were not really motivated by love but by selfishness (see Mark 12:38; also Matthew 23:27-28). Therefore, when He put so much emphasis on *agape* (God's love), the Pharisees realized He knew them far too well. His awareness of their true nature made them uncomfortable, and they decided to kill Him.

This same self-centered attitude was demonstrated at the Temple Treasury, where Jesus observed both rich and poor giving offerings (Mark 12:41-44). God is not satisfied with a token appreciation of love to Him – He requires our **whole hearts:**

"I know your works, that you are neither cold nor hot ... So then, because you are lukewarm (half-hearted) and neither cold (indifferent) nor hot (committed) to Me, I will vomit you out of My mouth.

"Because you say, 'I am rich, have become wealthy and have need of nothing (self-sufficiency)' – and do not know that you actually are wretched, miserable, poor, blind, and naked (lost without Me) – I counsel you to buy from Me gold refined in the fire (a life tested and purified) that you may be rich (in spiritual wealth), and white garments (Blood-washed, redeemed from sin by the salvation provided by Christ Jesus) that you may be clothed, that the shame of your nakedness may not be revealed; and anoint your eyes with eye salve (tune in to the things of the Spirit) that you may see."

Revelation 3:15-18; paraphrased

His Travel Itinerary

Directly and indirectly, Jesus had already confirmed to His disciples that He was indeed the Messiah, the Son of God, the Savior they had so long awaited. But they still did not understand. Now, in the last week of His human life, Jesus spoke plainly to them:

"When you see these things happening, know that [the end] is near, at the doors!

Assuredly I say to you, this generation will by no means pass away until all these things take place. Heaven and Earth will pass away, but My words will by no means pass away."

Mark 13:29-31

From the days of Moses until today, the Jews have been "reading signs" and watching for their promised Deliverer. Believers don't "look for signs" – they look for the Savior! **"Be alert, and keep praying,"** He instructed us. **"Do the work I have given you to do."** We want to be found faithful when He comes ... and **He might come today.**

Remember the Parable of the Ten Virgins found in Matthew 25:1-13. The bottom-line is:

"Watch therefore, for you know neither the day nor the hour in which the Son of Man is coming."

Matthew 25:10

Note: *"Watch and pray"* would now become a recurring theme, especially in Christ's ordeal in the Garden of Gethsemane. How did the disciples make out with obeying this command? How do we measure today?

When Jesus knelt to pray in the Garden, He truly was "between a rock and a hard place," facing the worst difficulty of His life.

The Joy of Giving

Backtracking a little, there is an important principle revealed in the part about people giving into the Temple Treasury:

Jesus sat down opposite the place where the offerings were put, and watched the crowd putting their money into the Temple Treasury. Many rich people threw in large amounts. But a poor widow came and put in two very small copper coins, worth only a few cents.

Calling His disciple to Him, Jesus said, "Truly I tell you, this poor widow has put more into the Treasury than ll the others. They all gave out of their wealth; but she, out of her poverty, put in everything – all she had to live on."
Mark 12:41-44

At some point in my childhood, I was taught this principle:

"That 'gift' which costs you little is a worthless gift. Giving out of your own need is what pleases God the most."

As a little girl, the first way I expressed this principle was when Christmas shopping: if I found a gift I really liked myself, I would buy it to give to someone else. It may have been as simple as a candle I thought was lovely and would like to have kept for myself, but I would give it away (and wait eagerly to see if that person liked it as much as I did). To this day, my favorite part of giving Christmas gifts is finding "that perfect something" for someone I love, and because I would personally enjoy having it, the act of giving it away is filled with anticipation of their joy at receiving it.

Learning that principle of "sacrificial giving" also led to the principle of the "joy of giving" ... which led to the enjoyment of "surprises" and "unexpected giving" (I'm not sure "surprises" is in the Bible). Then another concept cropped up: "pay it forward," meaning, *"If someone has given you something, then you plan to give something to someone else"* – such as being in a line-up at *Starbucks* and not only paying for your own *latté* but paying for the drink of the person standing behind you in line, who would not be expecting your generosity.

As for surprises, one of my favorite activities is planning an unexpected party for someone, such as a baby shower or an unanticipated element for a birthday party. In our extended family, the adults primarily celebrate the "decade years" (age 20, 30, 40, etc.) as significant milestones. To celebrate my husband Kenneth's 60th birthday in 2011, I researched extensively to locate his long-lost school-mates and friends from his youth, and invited them to join in a *"This Is Your Life"*-type party (special guests were assigned a specific decade to represent; then offstage, they queried him with clues as to their identities, which he had to decipher). It was all very mysterious, and Kenneth's surprise quotient was like an explosion of fun.

The *pièce de résistance* was having our son Alex – who is a missionary-teacher in India – fly halfway around the world (without Kenneth knowledge) just to be at his father's birthday party. Alex and his family even sent a "decoy" video that we aired, keeping the element of surprise alive as long as possible. (Sadly, Alex's plane was held over in Delhi due to fog, and he arrived 24 hours later than planned, thus missing the party. Still, Kenneth was honored by our efforts to surprise and celebrate him.)

These are some of the joys of giving, which come from a heart overflowing. The point Jesus was making was that the rich people were merely "tipping" God, no matter how grand their giving may have seemed to be; they were more about the outward appearance. But He could see directly into the heart of the poor widow, knowing that her heart was committed wholly to God, she put her trust in Him, and she was giving – not what she could afford – but everything she had. Like so many unsung people in Christian ministry, who work hard, live frugally, pour themselves out wholly, and serve faithfully.

But the Lord said to Samuel, "Do not consider his appearance or his height ... The Lord does not look at the things people look at. People look at the outward appearance, but the Lord looks at the heart."

1 Samuel 16:7

It is important to teach our children the covenant principle of tithing; it is equally important to explain that tithing is not an obligation – it is an act of love and gratitude. Then we must model over-the-top giving, which is above tithing; again, an act of love. We do not give to get – we give to bless others, to express our joy in living, and to honor our limitless Heavenly Father, Who gave us His very best in the gift of His own Son:

He who spared not His own Son but delivered Him up for us all, how shall He not with Him also freely give us all things?

Romans 8:32

Finally, as the old Pentecostal preacher always said, understand that we can never "out-give God." He doesn't need our "stuff," He only wants our hearts.

BIBLE QUIZ

(1).a) At the beginning of His ministry, who knew the true identity of Jesus Christ?

His Mother, Mary; and His cousin, John the Baptist.

(1.b) **Who did *not* recognize His true identity?**

The leaders of the Temple, and James, one of Jesus' half-brothers.

(2) **According to Passover tradition, for how many days was each family to examine their sacrificial lambs; and for how many days was Jesus "examined" in Jerusalem prior to the Feast of the Passover?**

Five days.

(3) **Complete this sentence: God is not satisfied with a _____ appreciation of our love to Him – He requires our _____ _____. (see Mark 12:41-44)**

*God is not satisfied with a **token** appreciation of love to Him – He requires our **whole hearts.***

Day 3 (Tuesday):
A Conference In Hell

BIBLE READING

Leaders Plot to Kill Jesus

After two days, it was the Passover and the Feast of Unleavened Bread. The chief priests and the scribes sought how they might take Him by trickery, and put Him to death; but they cautioned, "Not during the Feast, lest there be an uproar of the people."

Mary Anoints Jesus

While in Bethany at the house of Simon the leper, as Jesus sat at the table, a woman came having an alabaster flask containing very costly oil of spikenard. She broke the flask and poured the oil on His head. But there were some who were indignant among themselves, who complained, "Why was this fragrant oil wasted? It might have sold for more than three hundred denarii, which could be given to the poor." So they criticized her sharply.

Jesus answered, "Let her alone. Why do you trouble her? She has done a good work for Me. For you have the poor with you always; and whenever you wish, you may do them good.

"But Me you do not have always. She has done what she could. She has come beforehand to anoint My body for burial. Assuredly I say to you, wherever this Gospel is preached throughout the whole world, what this woman did will also be spoken of as a memorial to her."

Judas Plans to Betray Jesus

After this, Judas Iscariot, one of the Twelve, went to the chief priests to betray Him to them. When they heard it, they were glad and promised to give him money; then he sought how he might conveniently betray Jesus.

The Passover Is Prepared

Now on the first day of the Feast of Unleavened Bread, when they killed the Passover lamb, His disciples asked Jesus, "Where do You want us to go and prepare that You may eat the Passover?"

He instructed two of His disciples, "Go into the city, and a man will meet you, carrying a pitcher of water; follow him. Wherever he goes in, go and say to the master of the house,

'The Teacher says, "Where is the guest room in which I may eat the Passover with My disciples?"' Then he will show you a large upper room, furnished and prepared; there make ready for us."

So His disciples went into the city, and found it just as He had said to them; and they prepared the Passover.

Mark 14:1-16; paraphrased

BIBLE STUDY

[WARNING: This *fictional* segment might be too graphic for young children; use parental discretion.]

The Gruesome Chamber

The chamber was suffocatingly hot, dark, murky, occasionally illuminated by eye-stabbing flashes of lightning. A constant undercurrent of deep bass booming indicated that somewhere, someone – or something – was working steadily with a hammer and anvil, which then produced distant random screams of terror which echoed through the cavernous room.

An insidious slithering sound announced the arrival of a large frog-like being, and in its wake, a foggy red glowing mist began to infiltrate the chamber, revealing a huge, much-scarred table surrounded by mismated chairs. With a rumble, an enormous throne-like seat – mounted over an iron-barred cage packed with moaning humans – rose out of the filth-covered floor to wobble and float a few inches in the air.

A Horrific Cast of Characters

Suddenly, the atmosphere was charged with static electricity, and – without warning – each chair around the table was instantly occupied by grotesque creatures. Misshapen limbs, protruding features, clawing hands, hulking bodies or insubstantial apparitions – a wild array of beings who surrounded the table and cackled with sinister glee among themselves.

A huge sonic boom, and abruptly the throne at the end of the table was occupied. A suave, well-built, human-like creature sat there. Aside from the fact that his skin was a deep crimson color and he loomed about ten feet tall, he looked perfectly, handsomely human. His features were deceivingly striking good-looking, and he wore what appeared to be an expensive, black, three-piece business suit, *circa* third millennium AD, with a crisp white French-cuffed shirt, and a red silk – or was it snake? – tie that pulsated on his brawny chest. His neatly-manicured fingers strummed languidly on the arms of the chair. A large ring of metal keys hung on a belt around his slender waist. He appeared completely at ease, a private smile playing at his alluring lips. The creatures surrounding the table analyzed his mood ... and darted their eyes at each other uncertainly.

"Greetings, my warriors," the man-like creature spoke in an oily voice.

"Hail to thee, oh most terrible one!" ... "Greetings, most vile prince!" ... "Unholy Satan, we magnify thee!" **Satan!** The demon-beings around the table responded in deference with a variety of groveling oaths and inverted salutations. They awaited their profane master's next words with gloomy trembling.

A Grim View of History

"I have waited with incredible patience for this day," Satan began, his genteel countenance assuming a long-suffering expression. He idly stroked the keys on the ring at his belt. "From the day that I was ... er, cheated out of my, um, rightful standing in Heaven, throughout Human History I have waited for this day." The demons growled approval, recognizing their master's superb oration skills.

"Over and over again I have tried to take dominion of the Earth, and again and again God has thwarted my conquests." Hoary demon heads nodded knowingly. "But He finally ... made ... a ... mistake. One critically important mistake."

Titters of laughter shivered through the room. "Yes, one fatal error. For some silly reason, God allowed His very own Son to assume – oh, it is too ridiculous! – human form and live on Earth among people. And that very Son – once my arch-rival for all glory in Heaven – is now very, very vulnerable to me."

A screaming laughter now resounded. After it subsided, Satan continued in a mock-mournful tone, "Of course, I tried to stop Him when He was just a Baby." Commiserating moans were heard. Then Satan snarled, "You would think a helpless Child would be easier to kill! But no! His parents were forewarned of my scheme, and they whisked Him away to safety." His baleful eyes roamed the conference room. "But now ... He is walking right into my trap." The once-smooth countenance began to take on cruel planes as Satan was transformed into his natural milieu: a hideous, cast-out monster, with razor-sharp talons erupting from his fingers, wicked horns protruding from his temples, jagged fangs appearing in his evil grin, the tail of a dragon whipping furiously behind his throne.

Evil, approving chuckles were heard. From the cage beneath the throne, a murmur of sorrow issued. With mounting furor, Satan spoke each word distinctly, "Now ... I will ... destroy Him!" He roared, and a great cheer rose to the rafters of Hell. The captives imprisoned below began to weep.

The Fiendish Plot Unfolds

"I have a plan, a deliciously evil master-plan." Satan paused for a long moment, then slowly drawled, "I am ready to take your reports, my children. I am anxious to hear how my plan is proceeding." Beings fluttered ragged wings or shuffled scaly coils at their master's words. "Reports! Anyone? How about you, Lust?"

A creature with the head and face of a beautiful woman but the putrid body that displayed many arms, rose from its seat and hissed in self-defense, "My malicious lord, I ... I have nothing to report, your horridness. Believe me, I have tried diligently, but I have not been successful in tempting or overcoming the Son. He resists all my advances. He is my worst defeat!" It burst into self-pitying wails as it subsided into its seat, head lowered. Satan snarled at it with disgust, but waved a dismissing hand.

"Alright, then ... how about you, Greed? You generally are fool-proof."

A hulking creature, its wide mouth filled with countless sharp teeth, stood and bowed its decaying head. "No, your satanic majesty. I have not been effective against the Prince of Heaven either. He has never responded to my insinuations." Satan's eyes slitted with displeasure. Then Greed continued, "But! I have been successful in reaching one of His closest disciples!"

"Ah!" Satan smiled malevolently. "Good work, Greed! Which one have you attacked?"

"Judas Iscariot, the disciples' treasurer, my lord," Greed responded with satisfaction. "Already Judas has protested against certain wasteful practices that the Son has allowed. I am certain I will be able to use him more effectively soon, very soon."

A smattering of applause filled the room. Satan stretched his muscular torso and grinned, then caught his lashing tail and began to stroke it. "Well, at least that is a start. Anyone else?" The demon-masters conferred among themselves, then the fat frog-like creature, who had been first to appear in the room, stood up, puffing out a self-important chest and waving a thin-shanked arm.

"Yes, Religion? You have a report?"

"Oh mighty awfulness, my minions have been working overtime on your project, and they have performed disreputably. For the past three Earth-years, since –" here the creature stumbled and coughed – "Je- ... Je- ... Jesus of Nazareth began His public ministry, my legions of religion, controversy, pride, and false accusations have mounted a concentrated offensive against the Father's Son."

Other creatures murmured their approval, and Religions's inflated chest expanded even more, its many tarnished medals tinkling incongruously. "At first, we concentrated primarily on His home-town, where we had our first triumphs. We were able to arouse suspicion about His origins among His own kinsmen, reminding them to calculate the timing between His parents' marriage and the date of His birth."

Decadently mirthful laughs filled the room. "But we didn't stop there. When God's Son taught in the local Synagogue and declared

Himself the fulfillment of prophecy, it was not at all difficult to incite the populace, and eventually He was forced to leave."

A tiny, impatient frown had appeared on Satan's once-handsome face, and the fangs of his mouth appeared to grow longer. Noting these manifestations of impatience, Religion hurried, "When the Son left Nazareth and began traveling throughout Israel, I appointed my special forces to continually harass Him. Much of their accomplishments you already know, my master." It paused, and Satan nodded.

"I then infiltrated the San Hedrin, the religious rulers in Jerusalem, and assigned my strongest demons to mount a non-stop campaign into the ears of Caiaphas and Annas, the two high priests. Of course, they quickly succumbed to my suggestions that the Nazarene was a very real threat to them, both to their power-bases with the Jews and with the Romans, as well as a peril to their own personal status. It was not difficult to persuade them to join my harassing forces."

The Battle-Plan Revealed

Satan suddenly stood up and began pacing around the room. "So you, Religion, have been most successful in threatening the Son of God," he chewed his lip thoughtfully. Then he slammed his fist onto the conference table, sending sparks flying and startling the already-jittery demons. **"Now** is the time for the final attack! If we have sufficiently undermined His position, all of God's angels will not be able to protect Him from our ultimate assault!" Demons cheered, then subsided to listen with bated breath.

Satan returned to his throne and again sat regally upon it, closing his eyes. After a few moments, he slowly opened them, gazing at his gathered warriors, and smiling viciously. "Now, come forward, Confusion! Come forward, Hatred! Come forward, Murder! I require your services."

Three towering demons arose from the farthest end of the conference table, and lumbered toward the throne. Although they were all fellows in this nasty alliance, the other demons shrunk back from their smoky, odiferous passage. The three knelt at Satan's feet, awaiting their orders.

Satan was silent for a moment. "Long ago, a cursed prophet named Zechariah spoke. It is in ... The Book." All groaned with dismay, knowing this meant they were going to hear the Word of God quoted, a weakness which Satan exhibited with surprisingly frequency. "He said, *'I will strike the*

Shepherd and the sheep will be scattered'."
The demons then trembled with anticipation, awaiting the next words.

Satan bared his fangs. "It is **my right** to come against this despised Son once and for all! Even God has said that I may strike against Him. So now ... now is the time! We will attack Him, using surprise tactics to overwhelm Him!"

His voice rose shrilly, "Confusion, it is your time to send all your minions out. Send all your creatures, ordering them to hide in corners, in dark places, and wait to attack. Begin your mission now! We will catch Him unaware." Confusion nodded once, and instantly vanished. A distant rumble of thousands of running feet was immediately heard, and the crowd around the conference table grinned.

"Hatred, I command you to fill the hearts of men so thickly that there is no escape for the Son! Go at once, and plunge deep into them, becoming rooted to their souls. Spare no effort in establishing the atmosphere for the destruction that this final battle requires!" Demon fists pounded on the conference table with glee as the vile master of Hatred rose and slithered away. Another thunderous rumble was heard in the distance.

Satan leaned back in his throne and regarded the last kneeling demon. He paused, eyes slitted. Then he raised a brawny fist and held it high. "Murder, I unleash you to destroy the Son of God! **I want Him *dead!*"** He slammed his fist on the arm of his throne, leaving a significant dent. Then his hand streaked out and grabbed the demon by the throat: "I want His Body, understand?" Murder's throat gurgled, then it disappeared with a lightning crack. Satan sank back in his throne and howled a terrifying laugh.

A howling cheer resounded throughout Hell. A few lesser demons started running laps around the conference table, chanting: "We are going to kill Jesus! We are going to kill Jesus!"

The captives beneath the throne shuddered fearfully, huddling together in hopeless terror.

03

Jesus Was Prepared

Contrary to Satan's lofty opinion of himself and his "surprise attack" plans, in Mark chapter 14 we see Jesus was very prepared: for His betrayal, His burial, for fellowship, for danger, for death.

First, He was ready in advance for His burial. In Mark 14:2-9, the action of the woman (generally believed to be Mary Magdalene) with the alabaster flask was a haunting echo of the gifts which the Wise Men had brought at his birth (see Matthew 1:11).

The Controversy of Charity

It is interesting here to note how Jesus responded to the issue of charitable work. There are many today who believe it is better to give charitable donations to "good causes" – famine relief, homeless people, disease research – than to give tithes and offerings to God's House. Unfortunately, this attitude violates Scriptural principles badly, and will only lead to trouble (see Malachi 3:8-12).

In Matthew 6:1-4, Jesus encouraged *"the giving of alms"* (charitable acts or donations), but **never** in lieu of fulfilling your covenant with God, and never to receive the approval of men. There is a distinct Biblical order to the way we handle our pocketbooks: first, tithes to God; second, offerings to God's work; third, charitable acts or donations to the needy. If we don't put God first in all things, our "good works" are without lasting worth:

> *"Do not lay up for yourselves treasures on Earth, where moth and rust decay and where thieves break in and steal. But lay up for yourselves treasures in Heaven, where neither moth nor rust destroys and where thieves do not break in and steal.*

For where your treasure is, there your heart will be also."

Matthew 6:19-21

"Seek first the Kingdom of God and His righteousness, and all these things shall be added to you."

Matthew 6:33

It is also noteworthy that Jesus remarked, ***"The poor are with you always"*** (Mark 14:7). We will never see a class-less society, where there are no rich or poor, no advantaged or disadvantaged ... at least, not here on Earth. In Heaven, it's a different story for God alone is *"no respecter of persons"* (Acts 10:34). Therefore, no matter how great our motives may be, we will never be able to eradicate poverty and destitution from the Earth since they are both manifestations of the "evil fruit" of Satan's curse. That makes an even greater case for giving your money to the Lord's work before secular charities.

Please note: I do not say giving to charity is wrong. Just keep it in proper priority: **after** giving to God, **not instead** of fulfilling your covenant with Him. Many churches act as conduits for charitable giving, providing homeless shelters, free soup kitchens, blood-donation stations, schools, disaster relief, and so on.

Betrayal By a Friend

Jesus was prepared for betrayal. Although the chief priests had tried every trick (Mark 14:1) to trap Jesus into blasphemy or heresy, He had not succumbed. In order that God's ultimate plan would be fulfilled, He Himself allowed one of His hand-picked disciples and closest friends – Judas Iscariot – to become the tool which gave the religious leaders their opportunities.

His betrayal by Judas was permitted by God. Judas solved the high priests' problem by offering to lead them to Jesus when He was out of the public eye (Mark 14:10). But how does one "conveniently" betray the Son of God? Is there not an incredibly high price to pay for such an effort (see Matthew 27:5)?

Last Chance to Fellowship

Jesus also prepared for fellowship. It meant so much to Him to spend those last few hours with His beloved disciples, His best friends. He loved them (see John 13:1), and their presence encouraged Him. When Jesus sent two disciples to locate the "Upper Room" (remember the "secret signs" we discussed on Day 1?), He left no detail unattended. In this Room designated for guests, He intended to take the cup and bread of the Passover dinner and transform them into memorials of His own Blood and Body, for He wanted His disciples to remember Him and understand what He had done for them.

The Lord's Supper, which was prepared for the disciples that day, is one of the most significant activities which the Church enjoys today. More on this tomorrow.

ஒ~ஒ

BIBLE QUIZ

(1) **Complete this sentence: "If we don't put God _____ in all things, our 'good works' are _____ _____ _____."**

*"If we don't put God **first** in all things, our "good works" are **without lasting worth**.*

(2) **Memorize:**

"Lay up for yourselves treasures in Heaven, where neither moth nor rust destroys and where thieves do not break in and steal. For where your treasure is, there your heart will be also."

Matthew 6:19-21

(3) **Was Jesus prepared; if so, how?**

Yes – Jesus was totally prepared for His betrayal, His burial, for fellowship with His disciples, for the dangers of His arrest and trial, even for death. (see Mark 14)

Day 4 (Wednesday):
The "Full Meal Deal"

BIBLE READING

The Passover is Celebrated

In the evening, Jesus came with the Twelve. Now as they sat and ate, Jesus said, "Assuredly I say to you: One of you who eats with Me will betray Me."

They were shocked and sorrowful, and one by one they asked Him, "Is it I?"

Then Jesus answered, "It is one of the Twelve who dips with Me in the dish. The Son of Man indeed goes just as it is written of Him; but woe to that man by whom the Son of Man is betrayed! It would have been good for that man if he had never been born."

Christ Washes the Disciples' Feet

Now before the Feast of the Passover was ended, when Jesus knew that His hour had come that He should depart from this world to the Father, having loved His own who were in the world, He loved them to the end.

When Supper was ended (and the devil had already put it into the heart of Judas Iscariot to betray Him), Jesus – knowing that the Father had given all things into His hands and that He had come from God and was going to God – rose from Supper and laid aside His garments, took a towel and wrapped it around Himself. Then He poured water into a basin and began to wash the disciples' feet and to wipe them with the towel with which He was wrapped.

When He came to Simon Peter, he objected, "Lord, are You washing my feet?"

Jesus answered, "What I am doing you do not understand now, but you will know after this."

Peter again protested, "You shall never wash my feet!"

But Jesus responded, "If I do not wash you, you have no part with Me."

"Then, Lord," Simon Peter replied, "not just my feet, but my hands and my head as well!"

Jesus answered, "Those who have had a bath need only to wash their feet; their whole body is clean. And you are clean, though not every one of you" (for He knew who was going to betray him, and that was why He said not every one was clean.)

When He had finished washing their feet, He put on His clothes and returned to His place. "Do you understand what I have done for you?" He asked them. "You call Me 'Teacher' and 'Lord,' and rightly so, for that is what I am. Now that I – your Lord and Teacher, have washed your feet, you also should wash one another's feet. I have set you an example that you should do as I have done for you. Very truly I tell you: no servant is greater than his master, nor a messenger greater than the one who sent him. Now that you know these things, you will be blessed if you do them."

The Lord's Supper is Instituted

While they were eating, Jesus took bread, blessed it and broke it, and gave it to them, saying, "Take, eat; this is My Body." Then He took the cup, and when He had given thanks, He gave it to them and they all drank from it as He said, "This is My Blood of the New Covenant; which is shed for many. Assuredly I say to you: I will no longer drink of the fruit of the vine until that day when I drink it new in the Kingdom of God."

When they had sung a hymn, they went out to the Mount of Olives.

Mark 14:12-21; John 13:1-17; Mark 14:22-26; paraphrased

෨৵

BIBLE STUDY

To better understand what happened that Passover Night in the Upper Room in Jerusalem, we must go back to the beginning of The Book: to Exodus 11 and 12 (also remember what you read in the Preface of this book).

A Very Brief History

God's chosen people (the Children of Israel, or the Hebrews, or the Jews, or the Israelis – they had several titles) had become slaves in Egypt, and they desperately wanted to be liberated. God selected one of their very own: Moses ben Amram, of the Tribe of Levi; he was a Jew who had been raised incognito as a prince of Egypt. Moses was selected to become God's spokes- man to Thutmose II, the Pharaoh (the king of Egypt). Moses demanded Pharaoh release God's people, but Pharaoh was reluctant to lose several million valuable slaves. That refusal cost him and his nation heavily through a series of devastating plagues.

In the tenth and last plague, God unleashed the Angel of Death upon Egypt, killing the first- born of every family (except for the Jews, who had joined with God in a blood covenant to exempt them), slaughtering even Pharaoh's own crown prince. Finally, the devastated ruler released the Jews to their freedom.

Modern Parallels

Today, all those who put their faith in Jesus Christ are God's chosen people (see 1 Peter 2:9 and 1 Corinthians 6:20). The self-styled ruler of this Earth, Satan, still has Mankind in slavery. No one wants to be enslaved, and God's people are especially designated for freedom (see John 8:36 and Galatians 5:1). God's people **do** have a Deliverer (hand-picked by God Himself: His Divine Son, raised incognito on Earth), Who speaks on our behalf (see 1 John 2:1) ... and over two thousand years ago, He went nose-to-nose with that wicked ruler (see Revelation 1:18) and demanded that he let God's people go!

We too have a Blood Covenant with God Himself, one which causes the Angel of Death to be repelled by that very Blood which Jesus Christ offered on our behalf. That Blood not only covers our sins and removes them from God's sight, but it contains healing properties, protecting properties, restoring properties – it is an all-purpose Cleanser!

Jesus Has Always Been *"Mister Clean"*

John's account of the Last Supper contains an often-overlooked part of the story: the foot-washing scene (see John 13:1-17).

In those days, most of the streets of Jerusalem were unpaved, only compacted dirt, not graveled. Most people wore sandals, some wore boots, some simply wrapped their feet in strips of cloth, many went bare-footed. Travelers entering a house were asked to remove their foot-wear (if any) and wash their feet before proceeding indoors. In wealthier homes, a servant or slave was designated to perform this task. For the host to personally wash his guests' feet was a sign of tremendous honor (see Genesis 43:24).

By the third year of Jesus' public ministry, His hand-picked disciples were vicariously enjoying the popularity and notoriety of their Master, and likely had developed a sense of self-importance. Or perhaps they were so anxious to hear Jesus' teachings that they forgot the rules of common courtesy. Or possibly they were just uncouth men who never bothered with such niceties as feet-washing (although no self-respecting Jew would forego the hand-washing required by Jewish Laws; see Leviticus 22:6). Or possibly, because of the somewhat clandestine, "underground church" nature of the procurement of the Upper Room, they rushed indoors to avoid detection by those who hated Jesus.

In any case, when Jesus and His disciples arrived at the pre-arranged Upper Room, the Twelve rushed to the table and settled themselves for a meal ... forgetting to wash their feet or to assist their fellows. Can you imagine their embarrassment and surprise when their beloved Teacher stripped down His outer clothes (many slaves went naked or wore loin-cloths), wrapped a towel around Himself, poured water into a basin, and then humbly knelt to wash each of His disciples' feet!

As Jesus used ordinary water to wash His disciples' feet, this was a foretoken of the more-thorough cleansing He was about to complete with His life's Blood ... and the symbolic washing away of sins through the waters of Baptism.

"Come and Dine"

The Bibles tells of another banquet where guests were rude and ill-mannered. In Matthew 22:1-14, a king arranged a wedding feast for his son, and invited the rulers and nobility of many nations to attend. For one specious reason or another, none of them accepted the king's invit-ation. The insulted king then sent his armies to destroy his ungrateful neighbors.

Next, the king commanded his servants to go out to the public and invite everyone else – common people, sinners, bums, winos, outcasts, whoever they could find – to celebrate his son's wedding. Soon the king's banqueting hall was filled with a truly motley collection of people, all wining and dining at the king's table with great pleasure, cheering and toasting the groom and his bride.

However, when the king surveyed his strange assortment of guests, he noticed one man was not celebrating his prince's wedding but merely gobbling food. So the king had that man kicked out, saying, *"Many are called, but few are chosen"* (see Matthew 22:14).

The King's Banquet

Our Heavenly Father holds a Banquet every day in His House. All are welcome to enter and enjoy, but they must go through the washing part (see Hebrews 10:19-22) before they can be seated. As usual, Jesus Himself has made that provision for us, using His own Blood to remove the dirt of sin from us, gently wiping our tears of sorrow, and giving us clean robes of righteousness to wear when we stand face-to-face with the Father-King.

Then, when we sit down at the King's Table, there is an incredible array of dishes to enjoy! The "menu" is clearly described in several places in the Bible. First, we have menu options:

"If a son asks for bread, will his father give him a stone? Or if he asks for a fish, will he give him a serpent instead? Or if he asks for an egg, will he give him a scorpion? If you then, being wicked, know how to give good gifts to your children, how much more will your Heavenly Father give the Holy Spirit to those who ask?"

Luke 11:11-13

There is also a "children's menu":

As newborn babes, desire the pure milk of the Word, that you may grow thereby.
1 Peter 2:2

I fed you with milk and not with solid food, for until now you were not able to receive it.
1 Corinthians 2:2

You have come to need milk and not solid food. For everyone who partakes only of milk is unskilled in the word of righteousness, for he is a babe. But solid food belongs to those who are full age; that is, those who by reason of use have their senses exercised to discern both good and evil.
Hebrews 5:12-14

The basic food groups are served at God's Table. There is the *Bread of Life:*

"I am the Bread of Life. He who comes to Me shall never hunger, and he who believes in Me shall never thirst."
John 6:35

There is *Living Water:*

"Whoever drinks of the Water that I shall give him will never thirst. For the Water that I shall give him will become in him a

Fountain of Water springing up into everlasting life."

John 4:14

There is *Divine Wine:*

Do not be drunk with (earthly) wine, in which is dissipation; but be filled with the (Wine of the) Spirit, speaking to one another in psalms, hymns, spiritual songs, singing and making melody in your hearts to the Lord, giving thanks always for all things to God the Father in the Name of our Lord Jesus Christ.

Ephesians 5:18-20

There is *Everlasting Meat:*

Jesus answered them, "Most assuredly I say to you: you seek Me – not because you saw the signs – but because you ate of the loaves and were filled. Do not labor for the meat which perishes, but for the Meat which endures to everlasting life, which the Son of Man will give you because God the Father has set His seal on Him."

John 6:26-27

"My Flesh is Meat indeed, and My Blood is Drink indeed. He Who eats My Flesh and drinks My Blood abides in Me and I in him. As the living Father sent Me and I live because of the Father, so he who feeds on

Me will live because of Me."
John 6:53-57

There is *Holy Fruit:*

The Fruit of the Spirit is love, joy, peace, long-suffering, kindness, goodness, faithfulness, gentleness, self-control.
Galatians 5:22

Be filled with the Fruits of Righteousness, which are by Jesus Christ to the glory and praise of God.
Philippians 1:11

There is even a *Satisfying Dessert:*

He will feed His people also with the finest of wheat, and with honey from the Rock He will satisfy them.
Psalm 81:16

That is what I call a "Full Meal Deal"!

Children of the King

Although we feel unworthy
It's not the things we've done
That fit us for His Kingdom
But faith in Christ, His Son
His strength fills all our weakness
His life flows through our veins
He claims us sons and daughters
He loves us without shame

He is the King, the King of kings
And we are His Children
We walk by faith and not by sight
We are never alone
As children of the King of kings
Empowered by His Spirit
We can conquer in His Name

He sets His Feast before us
Don't linger at the door
Be seated at His Table
There's always room for more
We join our hearts to thank Him
We lift our hands in praise
This is the children's honor
To bless Him all of our days.

– Jeanne and Kenneth Halsey

The Lamb of God

As Jesus and His disciples ate the traditional Passover Supper of roasted lamb, unleavened bread, bitter herbs, and wine (see Exodus 12:8), He taught them many things (the four Gospels each detail that night with distinctly different perspectives). The common theme He carefully explained to His men (who still not grasp every-thing): *"I am the Lamb of God, and I willingly offer Myself as a Sacrifice for all men. I have come to die."*

How else could He tear a loaf of bread apart and offer it to His disciples, saying, *"Take, eat, this*

is My Body, broken for you. Do this in remembrance of Me" (Mark 14:22; also see 1 Corinthians
11:25) – unless His physical body was about to be
torn apart by executioners?

How else could He pour out the wine and pass
the cup around, saying, "Take, drink, this is My
Blood of the New Covenant, which is shed for
many. Do this in remembrance of Me" (Mark
14:23-24; also see 1 Corinthians 11:25-26) – unless His life's blood was about to stream out of His
body through wounds inflicted on His torso, head,
hands and feet, chest and side?

How else could they begin to **remember** Him –
unless He died and went away from them?

Jesus was the perfect Lamb (see 1 Peter
1:18-19) Who **had** to die to save us. We are
saved – not by admiring His example or by studying His teaching – but by applying His Blood to our
own hearts by faith. The Lamb saved the
Hebrews in Egypt and sustained them on their
journey. We "feed" on Jesus Christ when we
meditate on His Word, making it a part of our inner
persons.

Perfect Fulfillment

Josephus, a first-century Jewish historian,
reported, that there were **256,500 lambs** killed in
Jerusalem the year Jesus was crucified. With this
many lambs, it was necessary for the Jews to
prepare them (complete their examinations,

declaring them perfect and acceptable, then washing and grooming them) for sacrifice at **nine o'clock in the morning** of the fourteenth day of Nisan. They slaughtered and roasted them before three o'clock that afternoon so the Passover Dinner could be completed before six o'clock, which is traditionally the Jewish start of a new day.

At the exact hour when the Jews were preparing (slaughtering and then roasting) their lambs for sacrifice, Jesus was nailed to the cross. Mark wrote, *"Now it was the third hour, and they crucified Him"* (see Mark 15:25). The third hour was nine o'clock in the morning Jewish Time.

I Will Not Forget

More than a sacrifice, what You did that day
More than a substitute for debts we left unpaid
More than irrational, the love You felt for me
And I will not forget
More than obedience kept You in His will
More than kindness allowed Your blood to spill
More than compassion is how You are to me
And I will not forget

His precious blood was shed
A crown of shame upon His head
The limits of His love I'll never know
A sacrifice for every man
I don't pretend to understand
Just how far this Savior would go
For me, for you

More than a criminal, Your life knew no sin
More than a carpenter, our destiny within
More than a friendship, this brotherhood I've found
And I will not forget

More than merciful, the way You look at me
More than accepting, forgiving eyes don't see
More than a miracle, this single act of love
And I will not forget

You are my humble King
You are my everything
You are the song I sing
I will remember You.

– Michael Theriault

BIBLE QUIZ

(1) Who can come to the Father's Table and eat freely?

All who have first been washed by the Blood of the Lamb.
(see Hebrews 10:19-22)

(2) True or False: God's people are especially designated for freedom.

True. (see John 8:36 and Galatians 5:1)

(3) **When Jesus used ordinary water to wash His disciples' feet, this was a foretoken of what two things?**

The more-thorough cleansing He was about to complete with His life's Blood ... and the symbolic washing away of sins through the waters of Baptism.

(4) **Memorize:**

God made [Jesus] Who had no sin to become sin for us, so that in Him we might become the righteousness of God.

2 Corinthians 5:21

Day 5 (Thursday):
In the Garden and the Courts

BIBLE READING

Jesus Predicts Peter's Denial

When they had sung a hymn, Jesus and His disciples went out to the Mount of Olives. Then Jesus said, "All of you will be made to stumble because of Me this night, for it is written: 'I will strike the Shepherd, and the sheep will be scattered' (see Zechariah 13:7). But after I have been raised, I will go before you to Galilee."

Peter demurred, "Even if all are made to stumble, yet I will not be."

Jesus answered him, "Assuredly I say to you that today – even this night, before the rooster crows – you will deny Me three times!"

But Peter spoke more vehemently, "If I have to die with You, I will not deny You!" And all the disciples said likewise.

Jesus Prays in Gethsemane

Then they came to a place which was named Gethsemane; and He said to His disciples, "Sit here while I pray." He took Peter, James and John aside with Him, and He began to be troubled and deeply distressed.

He mourned, "My soul is exceedingly sorrowful, even to death. Stay here and watch!" He went on a little further, and fell on the ground and prayed, "If it is possible, may this hour pass from Me!" He cried, "Abba, Father, all things are possible for You. Take this cup away from Me; nevertheless, not what I will but what You will."

Then He returned and found Peter, James and John sleeping. He woke Peter, "Simon, are you sleeping? Could you not watch one hour? Watch and pray, lest you enter into temptation. The spirit truly is ready, but the flesh is weak."

Again Jesus went away and prayed as before. When He returned, He found them asleep again; for their eyes were heavy and they did not know what to answer Him.

Finally, He came the third time and asked, "Are you still sleeping and resting? It is enough! The hour has come; behold, the Son of Man is being betrayed into the hands of sinners! Rise up, let us go. See, My betrayer is at hand!"

Judas Betrays Jesus

While He was still speaking, Judas Iscariot – leading a great multitude of who came from the chief priests, scribes and elders, carrying swords and clubs – came into the Garden. Judas had pre-arranged a signal: "Whomever I kiss, He is the One; take Him and lead Him away safely." As soon as His betrayer approached, immediately he went up to Jesus and greeted Him, "Rabbi, Rabbi!" as he kissed Him. Then they laid their hands on Him and took Him.

Peter drew his sword and struck the servant of the high priest, cutting off his ear. But Jesus rebuked, "Put your sword in its place, for all who take the sword will perish by the sword" (see Revelation 13:10). Then Jesus touched the high priest's servant's ear and healed him.

Jesus continued, "Or do you think that I cannot now pray to My Father and He will provide Me with more than twelve legions of angels? (see Daniel 7:10) Have you come out as against a robber, with swords and clubs to take Me? I was daily with you in the Temple, teaching, and you did not take Me. But the Scriptures must be fulfilled; this is your hour, and the power of darkness."

Then the disciples all forsook Him and fled (including a certain young man who followed Jesus, who only had a linen cloth thrown around his naked body; when the mob laid hold of Him, he left the linen cloth and fled from them naked).

The San Hedrin Tries Jesus

They led Jesus away to the high priest, and with him were assembled all the chief priests, the elders and the scribes.

But Peter followed Him at a distance, right into the court-yard of the high priest, and he sat with the servants, warming himself at the fire.

The chief priests and all the Council sought testimony against Jesus to put Him to death, but found none. For many bore false witness against Him, saying, "We heard Him say, 'I will destroy this Temple that is made with hands, and within three days I will build another made without hands.' But not even then did their testimony agree.

So the high priest stood up in the midst and asked Jesus, "Do You answer nothing? What is it these men testify against You?" But Jesus kept silent and answered nothing. Again the high priest asked, "Are You the Christ, the Son of the Blessed?"

Jesus said, "I AM. And you will see the Son of Man sitting at the right hand of the Power, and coming with all the clouds of Heaven."

Then the high priest tore his clothes and wailed, "What further need do we have of these witnesses? You have heard the blasphemy! What do you think?" So they all condemned Him to be worthy of death.

Then some began to spit on Him, blindfolding Him and beating Him, taunting, "Prophesy!" And the officers struck Him with the palms of their hands.

Peter Denies Jesus

Now as Peter was below in the courtyard, one of the servant girls of the high priest came. When she saw Peter warming himself, she looked at him and remarked, "You also were with Jesus of Nazareth."

But Peter denied it, saying, "I neither know nor under-stand what you are saying." Then he went out on the porch, and a rooster crowed.

Then the servant girl saw him again and began to say to those who stood by, "This is one of them!" But Peter denied it again.

A little while later, those who stood by said to Peter again, "Surely you are one of them; for you are a Galilean, and your speech shows it."

But Peter began to curse and swear, "I do not know this Men of Whom you speak!" And a second time, the rooster crowed.

Then Peter called to mind the word Jesus had said to him: "Before the rooster crows twice, you will deny Me three times." When he thought about it, he wept.

Pilate Tries Jesus

Immediately in the morning, the chief priests held a consultation with the elders, scribes and the whole Council; and they bound Jesus, led Him away and delivered Him to Pilate. They began to accuse Him, saying, "We found this Fellow perverting the nation, and forbidding to pay taxes to Caesar, saying that He Himself is Christ, a King."

So Pilate asked Him, "Are You the King of the Jews?"

Jesus answered, "It is as you say."

Then Pilate said to the chief priests and the crowd, "I find no fault in this Man."

Bu they were more fierce, insisting, "He stirs up the people, teaching throughout all Judea, beginning from Galilee to this place." As soon as Pilate heard of Galilee, he asked if the Man were a Galilean. As soon as he knew that He belonged to Herod's jurisdiction, he sent Him to Herod, who was also in Jerusalem at that time.

Herod Tries Christ

Now when Herod saw Jesus, he was exceedingly glad (for he had desired for a long time to see Him, because he had heard many things about Him and he hoped to see some miracle done by Him). So Herod questioned Jesus with many words, but Jesus answered him nothing. The chief priests and scribes stood and vehemently accused Him. Then Herod, with his men of war, treated Him with contempt and mocked Him, arrayed Him in a gorgeous robe, and sent Him back to Pilate. (That very day, Pilate and Herod became friends with each other, for before that, they had been at enmity with each other.)

Pilate Tries the Christ Again

When Pilate had called together the chief priests, the rulers and the people, he gave his judgment: "You have brought this Man to me as One Who misleads the people. Indeed, having examined Him in your presence, I have found no fault in this Man concerning those things of which you accuse Him. And neither did Herod, for I sent you back to *him, and indeed nothing worthy of death has been done by Him. I will therefore chastise Him and release Him" (for it was necessary for him to release one of them at the Feast).*

But they all cried out at once, "Away with this Man, and release to us Barabbas!" (who had been thrown into prison for a certain insurrection made in the city and for murder).

Pilate, therefore, wishing to release Jesus, again protested Jesus' innocence to them; but they shouted, "Crucify Him! Crucify Him!"

For the third time, Pilate questioned, "Why? What evil has He done? I have found no reason for death in Him. I will therefore chastise Him and let Him go."

But they were insistent, demanding with loud voices that Jesus be crucified. The voices of these men and of the chief priests prevailed, so Pilate gave sentence that it should be as they requested. He released to them the one they requested (who for insurrection and murder had been thrown into prison) and delivered Jesus to their will.

Mark 14:26-47; Matthew 26:52-54; Luke 22:51-53; Mark 14:48-72; Luke 23:1-25; paraphrased

BIBLE STUDY

[This short story is fictional, but hopefully representative of how Heaven **might have been** perceiving the momentous events taking place on Earth.]

QUALIFYING ANGELS

"Oh, come on, Angela, you are being selfish!" Angela, the matriarchal angel, arched a single eyebrow at the petulant complaint of young Charlie, and waited for him to come to the proper conclusion himself. Which he did, after a few moments of fuming. "Well, alright, I know you've been given charge of the assignments – and there's no arguing with Him – but can't you bend the rules a little bit?"

Angela smiled serenely. "When it comes to the Prince, the King is very silent." A general mutter among Heaven's angels threatened, but she continued, "You heard the Prince say it Himself: *'Heaven and Earth will pass away, but My words will by no means pass away. But of that day and hour, no one knows, not even the angels of Heaven, but My Father only.'*" Angels all around her nodded reluctantly. "The King's plan is flawless. We must only wait it out, until it comes to the perfect conclusion."

"In the meantime …!" Charlie began, but Angela held up a restraining hand and he stopped. Then he gritted his teeth and grumbled, "Those ignorant humans always have a way of missing the main event! Remember those shepherds in the fields outside of Bethlehem? If we hadn't gone caroling ...." Again she held up her hand, and he bowed his head quickly. "Oh, alright."

Angela patted his shoulder, then addressed all the angels standing around listening, "There will be work for us to do, but it is not yet appropriate to inform you. Just be patient ... and exercise restraint. Whatever you observe occurring down on Earth, we must all conduct ourselves in proper angelic fashion. The Angelic Code is clear. Let us all recite it together."

Angels stood at attention, hands over their hearts, and began to recite:

Angels abide in Heaven.
Angels proclaim messages from God to people.
Angels obey God.
Angels are immortal.
Angels may guard the way of people.
Angels are not to be worshipped.
Angels may appear in dreams of people.
Angels go to Earth for special tasks.
Angels can be invisible.
Angels rescue God's people from danger.
Angels are awesome to behold.
Angels can perform miracles.
Angels protect children.
Angels worship God.

Angels can appear and disappear quickly.

At different points during the recitation, several angels nodded knowingly, or grinned delightfully, or nudged each other humorously. Remembering who they are and what their purpose is always seemed to settle the troops ... or so Angela thought. Then she grew serious, "Alright, now that we remember who we are and why we serve, I will tell you this." Expressions grew alert. "Shortly there will be several alarming developments in the Earthly life of the Son of God as He approaches His goal. He has fulfilled almost all the ancient prophecies, and the final days are near." Angels murmured, but she continued. "There is precise timing required for our participation in these last days, and all need to be on alert and ready at an instance's notice." She paused significantly, then continued.

"But ... I cannot tell you yet who will qualify and who will not. All I can say is: **be patient.** Our King knows what He is doing, and although it may not be understandable to us, still we are here to serve Him." She allowed this to penetrate. "Any questions?" No questions. "Alright, you are dismissed." The angels began to disperse. Angela looked around for Charlie ... and realized he was missing.

"Has anyone seen Charlie?" she asked before all the angels were scattered. Brief responses over their shoulders told her he was already gone … and she began to suspect he had been absent for quite awhile. "Charlie?" she called anxiously. "Charlie?" She rushed over to the enormous, gold-encrusted Celestial-scope mounted on a stand, and looked into it, pointing the lens down, sweeping it around. After a moment, she exclaimed, "Charlie!"

At that instant, a loud clap of thunder shook all of Heaven … and abruptly, a disheveled Charlie reappeared in a somersault, mist and dust drifting from his clothes. "Charlie!" Angela cried, rushing over and hauling him to his feet.

Charlie groaned, "I'm sorry, I'm sorry, I'm so sorry! I just could not resist."

"Oh, no, Charlie, what did you do?" Angela brushed at his robes.

Charlie slumped, "Well, I just happened to look … you know, look down on Earth, and I … I saw Him ... in trouble."

Angela was horrified, "What did you see?"

Charlie spoke reluctantly, "Well, the Prince was alone in a Garden, and He was talking with the King …"

"You eavesdropped on a private conversation between the Father and the Son?!?" she squeaked.

"No, not exactly … but I could tell by the anguished expression on His face, by the way He paused and listened, by the way His face fell … I just knew it wasn't good news He was hearing."

"So what did you **do**?"

Charlie began to sniffle, "Well, He was weeping … you know, such anguish of spirit that He was perspiring, and the sweat was like drops of blood … and so … so I took a handkerchief to Him, that's all."

Angela stood back and regarded the penitent angel with disbelief, "You went down to Earth and **ministered** to Jesus … without a permit?"

"I'm sorry, Angela! I know that was totally against the rules!" Charlie's face battled between remorse and defiance. "But He was weeping! His heart was breaking! I just **had** to help Him in some little way." He paused, reliving the whole experience. "And I don't think He really minded, not much anyway …."

At that point, another angel, Judith, rushed up to Angela. "Listen, Angela, listen! He's talking about us! Listen!" Judith went over to the Celestial-scope and fiddled with some buttons … and suddenly crackling through Heaven was:

"Peter …" It was the voice of the Prince!

"Who is Peter?" Judith whispered to George.

"He's that big, loud-mouthed disciple who is always putting his foot in his mouth and causing trouble," whispered George.

"Oh …," cringed Judith. "I wouldn't want that guy anywhere around here."

"Me neither. Slim chance he would ever be assigned any important duties in Heaven."

"Peter … put away your sword. All who use swords are destroyed by swords." Angels scurried in to hear the words of their beloved Prince. *"Don't you realize that I am able right now to call to My Father, and twelve companies of fighting angels – more if I want them – will be here, battle-ready?"* A great cheer went up at this, and

several angels flexed their muscles and growled ferociously.

"But *if* I did that ..." surprised expressions crossed many angel faces, *"how would the Scriptures come about that say this is the way it has to be?"*

Suddenly the audio transmission was cut off with a pop, and angels turned around to see two enormous angels – Gabriel and Michael – striding towards them. Instantly everyone stood to attention and saluted. Gabriel went to the Celestial-scope and touched a button thoughtfully, then looked into the lens.

Michael went to Angela, "Well, Angela, what happened?"

She completed her salute. "Oh, Michael, I'm so sorry. Charlie is ... a bit impetuous." Charlie cowered, and she put her arm around his shoulder.

Michael replied, "The King is ..." – Charlie shrunk even lower – "... not entirely displeased." A gasp went up all around, and Charlie's eyes grew wide. "But you broke the rules, of course."

Charlie cowered again, but a little smile – not a smirk! – toyed on his face. Angela rushed in, "Of course he knows the rules, and he is very, very sorry he broke them. He is greatly gifted with Compassion, you know, and it sort of overflowed unintentionally …."

Michael tried to look stern as he reached to lift Charlie to his feet. "One more stunt like that, young angel, and you'll be doing cloud-gathering duty for a millennium."

Charlie gulped, then straightened up. "Yes, sir. It won't happen again."

Gabriel finally withdrew from the Celestial-scope and touched another button. Then he looked around at the angels still standing to attention, and spoke, "At ease, Company A."

A great sigh went up among the angels as they stood down. Angela addressed Gabriel. "So what happens next, sir?"

Gabriel's expression was one of great sorrow. He chewed on his forefinger for a moment, then spoke to all. "The King has decreed that there shall be no more viewings of Earthly events on the Celestial-scope, until further notice." A shocked gasp ran through the angels, but they maintained discipline. "What is now unfolding on Earth is … not good … from our perspective. But from the King's viewpoint, it is exactly what He ordained, and nothing – **nothing!** – must interfere with its fulfillment."

Charlie dared to speak, "But the Prince said He would call twelve companies of battle-ready angels …"

Michael held up one finger. "He said, to be precise, that He **could** call for a legion of battle-ready angels … but He will not." A murmur of protest circulated, and the mighty Archangel held up all his fingers. "We … will … not … interfere, no matter what is happening down there." His expression grew very stern. "Is that understood? Company A, is that understood?" The angels nodded and stood quietly.

Angela spoke softly, as realization came, "So it is … the Ultimate Sacrifice?"

Gabriel nodded, and a tear trickled down his cheek. "Yes, this is it. The Prince is going to … die … for the sins of all Mankind. His is the Perfect Lamb of God, and He **will** take away all the sins of the world."

Charlie dared to speak again, "So He was weeping in the Garden because He is going to die?"

Michael answered, "No, child, that is not why the Prince was agonized." Puzzled expressions were everywhere. "He was realizing that the price He was about to pay requires Him – Who has never sinned in any way – to take **all** the sins of all the people for all time."

"I don't understand," whispered Charlie.

"When the Prince takes sin upon Himself, then the King will … no longer be able to look upon His Son … because the King hates all sin." Gabriel was fighting a strong emotion.

Angela too struggled with sorrow as she said, "So the Prince was weeping because He is about to be separated from the King as He chooses to take these sins on Himself."

Charlie asked, "And there is nothing we can do about it?"

Michael surprised everyone by smiling suddenly. "Ah, but there **will** be things for Company A to do!" Angelic countenances lifted. "There is more to come, after the sacrifice of the

Prince is complete." Excitement rippled through the assembly.

"Like what?" Charlie nearly bounced.

Michael laughed, "Grunt work, kid, grunt work! Stones to move, graves to open, veils to split, and then good news to proclaim … work like that."

Charlie looked perplexed. "'Graves to open'? Whose graves?"

Consulting a list, Michael read, "Hmm, first, there are the believers who died in faith … those guys, we'll open their graves for them …"

Gabriel put his hand on Michael's arm, "Hold it, my friend, don't tell them everything yet."

Michael looked a little chagrined; it was obvious his enthusiasm got the better of him. "Oh, right, sorry." He turned to the little angel, "You'll just have to wait for your assignment, kid."

But Charlie was not so easily dissuaded, "'Veils to split'? What does that mean?"

Gabriel now put his hand on Charlie's head, and the little angel subsided obediently. "You'll understand, my child, just let things unfold in God's timing."

The clever little angel made one last try, "So the Prince is going to die, but He is not going to remain dead, is that it?"

Gabriel and Angela laughed, as Michael chuckled, "You're about ready for a promotion, little one, because you can see, you can truly **see.** But don't rush ahead."

Charlie nearly danced with joy. "So I get to open the tomb for the Prince so He can get out?"

Angela smiled, "No, silly one, not so the Prince can **get out on His own** – He doesn't need our help for that – we'll be opening His grave so the people **can get in,** to see that … oh, never mind, that's not for you to know right now."

Suddenly a long thunder rumble sounded, growing louder and louder for what seemed an endless time, then slowly subsiding. Everyone stood stock-still. Then, a most unusual occurrence: it began to rain in Heaven. A light sprinkle misted all over the angels, and they were completely puzzled. Gabriel was first to understand and he put his hand over his mouth in dismay. He spoke softly, "The King is … weeping over His

Son." One by one, the angels sank to their knees. "It must be happening … now."

His Last Hours

The details of the last hours of Jesus' life are vividly portrayed in all four Gospels. Modern film-makers and dramatists have focused on the stress between a furious Simon Peter and a solemn Jesus of Nazareth, as they stood in the Garden of Gethsemane (see Mark 14:27-31, 66-72; also see Matthew 26:33-35, 69-75; Luke 22:31-34, 55-62; John 18:25-27).

Peter bravely boasts, *"I will never fail You, Master, not even if I am threatened with death!"*

Jesus answers, *"You will deny Me three times before this night is over"* – which Peter promptly does.

Why do you supposed each Gospel specifically mentions this betrayal of Jesus by one of His closest friends? Not every Gospel parallels each other precisely in details, yet this aspect of the story is considered important enough to duplicate four times.

Look around at our Christian leaders today. How many have failed the Master in some crucial hour? Too many. Yet it is not a new story. Throughout History, strong, sincere believers have faltered at the last minute again and again. Does Christ Jesus hold that against them? **No!**

Those who genuinely repent, ask forgiveness, try to repay their wrong to God and to Man, are indeed restored. On such people with "feet of clay" – as Simon Peter showed that fateful night – has the Kingdom of God been established. If God can forgive and restore, why cannot we?

Preparation for Death

Even as Jesus prepared Himself and His disciples for His ultimate betrayal, His burial and for danger, so He now entered the Garden of Gethsemane to face His final challenge: preparation for death. As we've studied before, Jesus willingly offered Himself as the Lamb of God, the Ultimate Sacrifice. He knew what He was doing from *"the foundation of the world"* (see Isaiah 28:16 and Revelation 13:8). Yet, He was troubled, and that deep anxiety is clearly detailed in Mark 14:33-42.

Why? Was He afraid of pain, afraid to die? He knew His betrayers and accusers would not be gentle with Him, would be as cruel and inhuman in killing Him as could ever be imagined. Did He love Life so much that the prospect of losing it caused Him to *"sweat drops of blood"* (see Luke 22:44)? No, Jesus was not afraid to die, nor feared the extreme pain and suffering His death would take.

This is what Jesus communicated with His Father:

"Abba, Father, all things are possible for You. Take this cup away from Me. Nevertheless, not what I will, but what You will."

Mark 14:36

Was He asking to be excused the responsibility of taking on all the sins of the world for all time? Was He asking for *"the cup of death"* to bypass Him? Was He asking to forego the shame, humiliation and defamation that He was destined to encounter? No, Jesus was not afraid of suffering.

Isaiah 53 was Jesus' "job description." It is one thing to be the Passover Priest (God the Father) and another to be the Passover Lamb (Jesus the Son). After He completed His job description (through death, resurrection and ascension), Jesus **became** that High Priest on our behalf:

Therefore, since we have a great High Priest Who has ascended into Heaven, Jesus the Son of God, let us hold firmly to the faith we profess. For we do not have a High Priest Who is unable to empathize with our weaknesses, but we have One Who has been tempted in every way, just as we are – yet He did not sin. Let us then approach God's Throne of Grace with confidence, so that we may receive mercy and find grace to help us in our time of need.

Hebrews 4:14-16

Jesus surrendered His life in the Garden of Gethsemane **before** He was arrested. No one took His life from Him – He had already given it. He never panicked throughout His trial of arrest, beatings, abuse, or crucifixion.

Breach of Fellowship

Jesus was not afraid of any of these terrifying aspects of His soon-coming death, He was not even fearful of taking on our sins. Jesus was dreading the experience of something He had never known in His entire existence: **the severing of fellowship with His Father. JESUS AGONIZ-ED OVER THE INEVITABLE SEPARATION FROM GOD.** Since the Fall of Adam and Eve, this is precisely what the condition of Mankind has been: **we are separated from our Father God.**

God cannot abide sin. He sees it from afar ... He despises it ... He rejects it. He destroys sin. Yet His assignment for His only Son was to **become** sin:

*God made Jesus, Who knew no sin, to **be** sin for us, that we might become the righteousness of God in Christ.*

2 Corinthians 5:21

When we read that the whole verse carefully, we see that there was an agreement, a contract, a covenant between God and His Son. God **required** that Jesus become sin. That was God's part: to allow His only begotten, most beloved Son to take on all the characteristics of despised sin. Jesus' part was to become sin **so that we might be restored to our Father.** What an agreement!

No, I don't believe Jesus was having second thoughts about torture and death. I believe Jesus was dreading separation from God, which is the death – not of the body – but of the spirit. He had never known "no contact" before, and He dreaded it above all else.

God destined Man to be His companion. He created us to fellowship with Him, to worship and love Him, and for He to love us. He fashioned us to receive His love and tenderness, His pleasure in us. He formed our spirits with a portion within where only He can fit.

There is a God-shaped vacuum in the heart of every person, and it can never be filled by any created thing. **It can only be filled by God,** *made known through Jesus Christ.*

— **Blaise Pascal,** *"Pensees"* (1670)

When Adam and Eve sinned in the Garden of Eden, that fellowship was broken. We became unplugged from Him. From that day in Eden to that night in Gethsemane, Man was condemned to be forever separated, disconnected from God the Father. There was only one way to get reconnected, and that was Jesus' part of the transaction.

Although we might try everything else – alcohol, drugs, money, power, sex, fame, sin, even "good works" – nothing or nobody else fits into that "God-shaped core" of our hearts but God Himself. The only way we can re-enter that fellowship with the Father is through the sacrifice of His Son Jesus. That's a lot of weight for One Man to carry!

He Paid A Debt

He paid a debt He did not owe
I owed a debt I could not pay
I needed Someone to wash my sins away
And now I sing a brand-new song
Amazing Grace
Christ Jesus paid the debt that I could never pay.

– Mylon LeFevre

Still the Disciples Slept

Here we witness Jesus going through the most difficult trial of His life ... and His faithful companions were right beside Him, praying fervently. Right? Wrong! There was no cute little sleep-fairy tiptoeing around the disciples, sprinkling little sparkles of sleep-dust into their eyes and soothing them to sleep with a sweet lullaby. I believe it must have been that deceptive demon of Apathy – which still plagues so many churches today.

One modern representation of the disciples in the Garden of Gethsemane depicts them drunkenly clutching their wine-skins and nodding off into alcohol-induced stupors. It is certain they had full bellies from the Passover Supper, and the Bible records they **had** consumed wine, and it *was* the middle of the night. But their inability to travail in prayer with their precious Master was more than just "natural slumber": I believe they were in the grip of that same demon who knows how to croon impassivity, indifference, "Let someone else do it ..." into our own ears today.

Hadn't Jesus warned them – and us – about this? *"Take heed, watch and pray, for you do not know when the time is"* (see Mark 13:33)? Fellow-believers: fight against that temptation to sleep in on a Sunday morning! Reject that desire to watch television rather than attend a prayer meeting! Keep your commitment to support that missionary in their outreaches! Stay alert! Be busy doing the Father's work!

The Last Miracle

The first miracle Jesus ever publicly performed was to transform water into wine at a wedding (see John 2:1-11). He did this out of compassion for the celebrants – not because they asked Him (although His mother asked Him), or because He felt obliged, but because He wanted nothing to diminish their joy in the wedding. He was compassionate.

The last miracle Jesus publicly performed was to heal the amputated ear of the high priest's servant (see Mark 14:43-39). Again, Jesus was not asked by the servant to do this, nor was He obliged to this man who was simply fulfilling his duty. The servant was likely innocent of any wrong-doing or malice. Jesus felt compassion for him, and although He was facing a hateful, muttering crowd, although the tension was mounting, He still took the time to reach out His hand to heal and restore.

This same kind of compassion would be evidence while He hung on the cross. This same kind of compassion is extended to His people today:

Jesus Christ the same, yesterday, today, and forever.
Hebrews 13:8

Jesus is Tried By His Own People

For three years, the priests, Pharisees and Sadducees tries to get evidence against Jesus that would empower them to put a stop to His ministry. They tried bribery, trickery, subterfuge – nothing worked. Jesus outsmarted them every time. But now – because He **allowed** it in order to fulfill the bargain with His Father – Jesus deliberately walked right into their hands.

They could not arrest Him in public. They had to wait until the middle of the night, when He was alone in a private place, away from the general populace who loved Him. They manhandled Him roughly. They hastily gathered as many of the religious officials and stool-pigeons as they could find, to bring Him to trial:

> *They led Jesus away to the high priest, and with him were assembled all the chief priests, the elders and the scribes. ... All the Council sought testimony against Jesus to put Him to death, but found none (for many bore false witness against Him, but their testimonies did not agree).*
> **Mark 14:53-56**

Blasphemy was finally the shaky (and untrue and unproven) charge they trumped up against Jesus *"... and they all condemned Him to be deserving of death"* (Mark 14:64-65).

Under the laws of Roman occupation, all Jewish civil laws were suspended – although they were permitted to exercise their religious laws. Equally, under Jewish religious restrictions, if the Pharisees were to put a man to death during the Passover, they would become ritually unclean and so be unable to participate in the Feast of the Passover. Therefore, when the San Hedrin needed a warrant to execute Jesus, they had to turn to the Roman government (as represented by Pontius Pilate) for help.

Jesus is Tried By the Highest Contemporary Authority

An angry crowd of furious priests, enraged scribes, heated informants (whose "evidence" had been very contradictory), agitated soldiers, and frenzied onlookers marched a manacled Jesus through the night streets of Jerusalem, to the Roman garrison. Pilate's initial concern was not the charge of blasphemy – because he wouldn't have considered the violation of bizarre Jewish religious laws very important anyway – but of possible insurrection: if Jesus claimed Himself to be the "King of the Jews," then He was setting Himself up in opposition to Rome, and that **was** a punishable offense. (Plus Pilate already had one insurrectionist in prison at this time: a man named Barabbas.)

With the calm of a practiced legal mind, Pilate ignored the fury of the crowd and asked Jesus straightly, "Are You the King of the Jews?"

Jesus – Who knew no sin and cannot lie (see Numbers 23:19) – correctly answered, *"It is as you say."* He would not, could not, deny His rightful heritage; neither would He say the expedient lie that might help Him escape execution. And although His own race began to scream accusations against Him, Jesus answered them not at all.

Pilate's analysis: *"I find no fault in this Man"* (Luke 23:4). Pilate gave Jesus an opportunity to refute His accusers, and he marveled at His composure. The more silently Jesus stood, the more enraged the howling crowd became. Popularity was not really an issue with Pilate; he did not care what the angry mob demanded: he was going to abide by the letter of the law. And his conclusion remained: *"I find no fault with this Man."*

Finally, Pilate overheard a tidbit that offered an escape from an increasingly ugly situation. One accuser had screamed, *"He stirs up the people, teaching through all Judea, **beginning from Galilee,** to Jerusalem"* (Luke 23:5; emphasis added). When Pilate realized Jesus hailed from Galilean jurisdiction, he conveniently decided to "pass the buck" onto Herod, who was the puppet-king of Galilee (the actual – although despotic – heir to the title, "King of the Jews").

Jesus is Tried By His Old Enemy

Once again, Jesus was delivered to the rough hands of an angry rabble and trundled off to King Herod's lodgings in Jerusalem, who was visiting for the Holy City.

Contrary to Pilate ambivalence – he found the whole situation disagreeable – Herod was the one person who was actually glad to see Jesus that night. This Herod was the grandson of the earlier King Herod who had once ordered the massacre of all the babies in Bethlehem, in an attempt to kill the Son of God (Jesus). What his grandfather failed to accomplish, this Herod now had opportunity to complete. (This Herod was also the easily-offended ruler who arrested and then executed Jesus' cousin John ben Zacharias, known as "the Baptist.")

With the degenerate pleasure of an consumingly carnal man, Herod viewed Jesus coming to him as an unexpected fortuity. He would see for himself, at his own convenience, some of the "tricks" which the famous Teacher could "perform." He had no interest in justice ... he did not take the charges of "self-proclaimed King of the Jews" seriously (although it was his own throne that was at stake) ... he was not responsive to the mob mentality. He certainly was not a believer or follower of Jesus as the Messiah, but merely viewed Him as an interesting charlatan, Who could possibly entertain his jaded senses for a time.

Also unlike the somber response of Pilate, Herod teased and taunted Jesus, making light of both the blasphemy and insurrection charges. When Jesus refused to respond, Herod peevishly lost his temper and mockingly ordered that Jesus be "properly attired" as the so-called "King of the Jews," with a royal robe ... and a royal crown: a crown woven of needle-sharp thorns, which was then jammed down hard upon His head, digging bloodily into His skull. Then, in a typically decadent fashion, Herod lost interest in the whole proceeding and dismissively ordered that Jesus be returned to Pilate for "final disposition."

Once again, Jesus was spared from the murderous hand of a Herod.

The Final Solution

By now, the light of Friday morning was dawning. It had been a wearying night. Jesus had last eaten with His disciples many hours before, in the Upper Room. He had not slept. He had spent several agonizing hours in prayer.

He had been repeatedly surrounded by a seething, angry mob ... had been arrested ... screamed at ... spit up ... manacled. He had been unjustly tried by hate-filled people intent upon His death.

He had been investigated by the highest authority in the land ... and then passed off to another (lesser) authority who only maligned Him. He had been abused ... and now wore a circlet of piercing thorns around His forehead and scalp; blood streamed unchecked down His face.

At this point, He was marching in yet another bureaucratic parade, and – although He was surrounded by a military escort – the derisive shouts and screams of an increasingly violent throng assaulted His ears. Jesus was shoved into Pilate's judgment hall again, where He stood swaying with weariness, pain and sorrow, appearing before a disgusted official who really didn't want to deal with Him.

"I find no fault in this Man," was still Pilate's response. *"But he knew that the chief priests had handed Him over because of envy,"* states Mark 15:10. What was one silent Man compared to the angry, envious insistence of the elders and patri- archs of the whole city?

The howling mob – composed, at least, of the boisterous citizens of Jerusalem who had once welcomed Jesus with such joy, but peppered with the falsehood-bearing minions of the San Hedrin – now demanded His death. In exchange for the release of a popular criminal (Barabbas), they cried out for the cruelest, harshest, most demeaning penalty of their day: crucifixion.

Jesus – the spotless, sinless Lamb of God – not only exchanged His life for Barabbas – a wicked rebel and heartless murderer – that day ... He exchanged His life for **all of Mankind.**

ॐ

Three Demon Legions

Three legions of demon-soldiers – under the command of Confusion, Anger and Murder – had thoroughly infiltrated the Jerusalem mob, and had done their work with exceptional success. Their scaly throats were hoarse and rasped from hours of screaming, "Crucify Him! Crucify Him!" – and now they triumphantly slithered back into Hell, their part of the grand plan accomplished.

BIBLE QUIZ

(1) Does God ever forgive people who have committed terrible sins?

Yes! Anyone who genuinely repents (stops and turns away from sin), asks forgiveness, and commits to obeying God, is indeed forgiven and restored.

(2) Why did Jesus agree to "become sin"?

*Jesus agreed to become sin, once and for ever, so that **we** might be restored to our Heavenly Father. (see 2 Corinthians 5:21)*

(3) What were the three levels of "authority" that put Jesus Christ on trial, what were their motives and what were their verdicts?

(i) The San Hedrin, the Jewish religious authorities, brought false charges and dishonest testimony against Jesus, and eventually found Him "guilty" of blasphemy. Their motive was to secure their own positions and to seek His death. They sentenced Him to death (but did not have the authority to carry out the sentence).

(ii) King Herod, the Jewish political authority, could not find any fault in Jesus at all. He descended from a long

line of "Herods" who had unsuccessfully tried to destroy the Son of God before; his motive was revenge. Herod had Him beaten according to Jewish custom (39 stripes) and a crown of thorns jammed onto His head, but powerlessly sent Him back to Pilate.

(iii) Pontius Pilate, the Roman governor, could not find any fault in Jesus, and he wanted to release Him. His motive was to free Jesus, but he also had to placate the local religious leaders. At first he ordered that Jesus be whipped and released; later he offered the Jewish mob a choice between two prisoners (which was a custom at Passover) and so acquiesced to the howls of the crowd to release Barabbas and crucify Jesus.

(4) **Memorize:**

Jesus Christ the same, yesterday, today, and forever.
Hebrews 13:8

Day 6 (Good Friday): D-Day

BIBLE READING

The Lamb of God Foretold

Who has believed our report, and to whom has the arm of the Lord been revealed? For He shall grow up before God as a tender plant, and as a root out of dry ground. He has no form or comeliness, and when we see Him, there is no beauty that we should desire Him. He is despised and rejected by men, a Man or sorrow and acquainted with grief. We hid, as it were, our faces from Him; He was despised, and we did not esteem Him. Surely He has borne our griefs and carried our sorrows; yet we allowed Him to be stricken, smitten by God, and afflicted.

He Was a Willing Sacrifice

But He was wounded for our transgressions, He was bruised for our iniquities, the chastisement for our peace was upon Him, and by His stripes we are healed. All we like sheep have gone astray; we have turned, every one, to his own way; but *the Lord has laid on Him the iniquity of us all.*

He was oppressed and He was afflicted, yet He opened not His mouth. He was led as a lamb to the slaughter; and as a sheep before its shearers is silent, so He opened not His mouth. He was taken from prison and from judgment; and who will name His offspring? For He was cut off from the land of the living; for the transgressions of God's people, He was stricken.

His Glorious Reward

And they were going to make His grave with the wicked, but instead buried him among the rich because He had done no violence nor was any deceit in His mouth. Yet it pleased the Lord to bruise Him; He has put Him to grief. And since **God made His soul an offering for sin,** He shall see His seed, He shall prolong His days, and all the pleasure of the Lord shall prosper in His hand.

God shall see the travail of His soul and be satisfied. By His knowledge, My righteous Servant shall justify many, for He shall bear their iniquities. Therefore I will divide the spoil with the strong because He poured out His soul unto death and was numbered with the transgressors. He bore the sins of many, and made intercession for the transgressors.

Jesus is Condemned By Man

Then Pilate said to the mob, "What evil has Jesus done?"

But they cried out more exceedingly, "Crucify Him!"

So Pilate – wanting to gratify the crowd – released Barabbas to them, and he delivered Jesus (after he had scourged Him) to be crucified.

Jesus is Beaten

Pilate's soldiers took Jesus into the Praetorium, and gathered the whole company of soldiers around Him. They stripped Him naked, and put a scarlet robe on Him; and made a crown from long thorns and rammed it on His head; and placed a stick in His right hand as a scepter, and knelt before Him in mockery. "Hail, King of the Jews!" they yelled. And they spit on Him, and grabbed the stick and beat Him on the head with it.

After the mockery – when they finally tired of their sport – they took off the royal robe and put His own homespun garment on Him again, and took Him out to crucify Him.

Jesus is Crucified

As they were on the way to the execution grounds, they came across a man from Cyrene (in Africa) – Simon was his name – and forced him to carry the cross of Jesus. Then they went to an area called Golgotha (that is, "Skull Hill") where the soldiers offered Him drugged wine to drink; but when He had tasted it, He refused. Then, at about nine o'clock in the morning, they crucified Him.

Jesus is Scorned

While He was suffering, the soldiers threw dice to divide His clothes among themselves. Then they sat around and watched Him as He hung there. Jesus said, "Father, forgive them, for they don't know what they're doing." Then they put a sign-board above His head that detailed His "crime," sarcastically adding: "This is Jesus, the King of the Jews."

Two robbers were also crucified there that morning, one on either side of Him (in this way, the Scripture was fulfilled that said, "He was counted among evil men"). And the people passing by hurled abuse, shaking their heads at Him and saying, "So! You can destroy the Temple and build it again in three days, can You? Well then, come on down from the cross if You are the Son of God!"

Jesus is Mocked

The chief priests and Jewish leaders also mocked Him. "He saved others," they scoffed, "but He can't save Himself! So You are the King of Israel, are You? Come down from that cross, and we'll believe You! He trusted God ... let God show His approval by delivering Him! Didn't He say, 'I am God's Son'?" And the robbers also threw the same in His teeth.

That afternoon, the whole Earth was covered with darkness for about three hours, from noon until three o'clock. At about three o'clock, Jesus shouted, "Eli, Eli, lama sabbach-thani" – which means, "My God, My God, why have You forsaken Me?" Some of the bystanders misunderstood and thought He was calling for Elijah.

One of them ran and filled a sponge with sour wine, put it on a stick and held it up to Him to drink. But the rest said, "Leave Him alone. Let's see whether Elijah will come and save Him."

The First Salvation Response

One of the criminals hanging beside Him scoffed, "So You're the Messiah, are You? Prove it by saving Yourself ... and us too, while You're at it."

But the other criminal now protested, "Don't you even fear God when you are dying? We deserve to die for our evil deeds, but this Man hasn't done anything wrong." Then he turned to Jesus and asked, "Lord, remember me when You come into Your Kingdom!"

Jesus replied, "Today you will be with Me in Paradise. This is a solemn promise."

Jesus' Job is Completed

By now it had been dark for about three hours. The light from the sun was gone – and suddenly, the thick veil hanging in the Temple split apart. The Earth shook, and rocks broke, and tombs opened, and many Godly men and women who had died came back to life again.

Then Jesus shouted, "Father, I commit My Spirit to You! It is finished!" ... and with those words, He died.

When the Roman centurion (the head of the military unit handling the execution) saw what had happened, he was stricken with awe before God, and exclaimed, "This Man was innocent! Surely He was the Son of God!"

Isaiah 53, paraphrased; and a **Composite of all four Gospels;** emphasis added

꧁꧂

BIBLE STUDY

[Another **fictional** short story, indicating how secular people may have perceived the sacrifice of Jesus Christ.]

A CRUCIFIXION PERSPECTIVE

My name is Marcus Atillio. I am a Roman soldier on deployment to Israel, one of the toughest nations in the entire Roman Empire. This month, I have been assigned to crucifixion detail in Jerusalem, their capitol city. This is one of the worst assignments a soldier can have; we have already crucified dozens of Jewish people this year alone. Today we are going to crucify three Jewish men.

Two are convicted thieves; I was there when one was captured so I know he was guilty. Don't know much about that second one. The third man has been convicted of breaking the Jewish laws and perhaps some kind of treason against the Roman government; the witnesses said He claimed to be the King of the Jews, but I don't really believe their charges. However, my centurion says I have to perform my duties – after all, how well I per-form is part of my military record – and so I will take all three prisoners through the city of Jerusalem and out to the usual execution site, a place called the Hill of Golgotha.

When we arrive at Golgotha, I will make all three prisoners strip off all their clothes; all convicted criminals are naked when they are executed, it's part of the humiliation process. Not that they have much in the way of clothing left after the beatings they will have been given. They will already be in a lot of pain from the whippings and torture they have been through. I'm glad I was not on beating-and-torture assignment this month; that's not a part of soldiering that I enjoy.

Each prisoner carries the crossbeam of his own execution instrument out from the city. My job is to attach the crossbeam to the upright posts that are waiting for them, laying on the ground, ready to be used again. We attach the crossbeam by hammering six-inch-long iron spikes from the front and the back of the upright posts. Then we make the prisoners lay down on the now-formed crosses, force them to stretch their arms out along the width of the crossbeams, tie their wrists to the crossbeams, and then I use more of the long spikes to secure their hands to the wood. This is very, very painful for the prisoners … but since they have been condemned to death, I try not to be overly concerned about their problems or feelings. Next I cross their legs at the ankles, tie their feet down, and drive a longer spike through their feet to secure them to the upright posts. Finally, we use ropes and pulleys to raise the crosses upright, and drop them into the holes that have already been dug. That's it ... except we have to wait for the prisoners to die.

Today my crucifixion detail leader, Centurion Maximus, has given all of us strict orders to keep the rabble away from the crosses. He says there are many Jews who hate that third prisoner who was accused of treason, and they might cause riots. I hope not – I don't like to get into fights with civilians. Although it seems a bit strange, my primary job is to guard the dying men, especially that one in the middle.

Awhile ago, the middle prisoner said He was thirsty and asked for a drink of water. We have a numbing drug in the vinegar-water mix which we are allowed to give prisoners; it helps them forget some of the pain. But when He tasted it, he spat it out. I'm sure He was in a lot of pain; I don't know why He did that. Just now, He looked at me and I heard Him say something that I really do not understand. I think He said, *"Father, forgive them, for they don't know what they are doing."* I can't be sure since He spoke Aramaic, and I'm still learning the language. Do I need to be forgiven? I don't know. I'm just doing my job.

I'll be glad when this detail is over tonight. I don't feel very well. The sky keeps getting darker and darker; I think a big storm is coming. All the people watching these executions are very agitated; some of them are weeping, others are shouting insults. I hope these three men will hurry up and die. That one in the middle is certainly bleeding a lot; I think He will probably bleed to death soon.

I hope my next assignment is something less gruesome, something more worthy of a true soldier. I admit I feel sorry for the family of that man in the middle. I'm not supposed to care about these people, or the ones I execute, but something inside me hurts a lot right now.

ങ

Slaughtering the Lamb

Three times Jesus Christ, the Son of God, was tried by men. The first trial was conducted by men intent on His death; the second trial (in two parts) was conducted by a man intent on His freedom; and the third trial was conducted by a man intent on greed and revenge. Jesus Christ, the Lamb of God, was executed by crucifixion – the most brutal, torturous death ever devised by men (and one "circumstantially" similar to the orthodox ritual of lamb-slaughtering) – a sentence reserved for slaves, thieves and traitors.

An Innocent Bystander

Do you remember Simon Peter's brash insistence that he would do **anything** for Jesus, would **always** be there for Him, would even give up his own life for the Master? Don't you think it should have been Simon Peter as the brawny guy picked out of the crowd by the Roman soldiers, to shoulder the cross of Jesus and carry it to Golgotha? Instead, it was a different Simon: Simon of Cyrene, a total stranger – an out-of-town visitor unexpectedly tagged for this grisly parade duty – who was forced to perform this heavy responsibility.

There is really not much known about Simon of Cyrene. Scholars speculate he was probably a Negro, since Cyrene is in Africa. He may have been a Jew who had made the pilgrimage to Jerusalem for the Holy Days. Or he may have been a Gentile who was simply "at the wrong place at the wrong time." But there was something special – perhaps something dependable and steady – about him that he would be noticed in the crowd and so come to the attention of the Roman soldiers.

There are many today who boast about their steadfastness and strength as a Christian, who insist they would gladly suffer a martyr's death for their Lord. (We do have the benefit of latter knowledge that there are special crowns in heaven for martyrs; see James 1:12.) But God, in His wisdom, often overlooks the loud-mouth and chooses the soft-spoken instead.

Jesus Christ said:

"Come unto Me, all you who labor and are heavy-laden, and I will give you rest. Take My yoke upon you and learn from Me, for I am gentle and lowly in heart, and you will find rest for your souls. For My yoke is easy and My burden is light."
Matthew 11:28-30

Probably unknowingly, Simon of Cyrene truly fulfilled Jesus' command that day, and became the first person to literally *"take up My cross and follow Me"* (see Matthew 16:24 and Mark 10:21).

The Thirty-Nine Stripes

Along with personal slandering and vile defamation, Jesus was physically abused repeatedly before He was subjected to the ultimate cruelty of crucifixion. The mob in the Garden of Gethsemane manhandled Him.

In the ground-breaking movie, *"The Passion of the Christ,"* I was startled that the film-makers showed Jesus being punched and beaten within moments of being arrested in the Garden of Gethsemane. While the Temple soldiers are marching Him to the first trial, His face is attacked so badly that His right eye becomes swollen and bruised immediately. Jim Caviezel, the outstanding actor portraying Jesus, reported that putting on the make-up and prosthetics for these scenes was so arduous and time-consuming that he often kept it all on overnight, even sleeping with it on. That brought such a dramatic vision to my under-standing of how brutally He was treated, especially by His own people.

It was at the third trial – conducted by Herod (the direct descendant of the old, old enemy of the Christ) – where He was whipped according to Jewish Law ... and where the most miraculous "coincidence" occurred. In those days, both Romans and Jews had specific guidelines for whipping or scourging. Under Jewish Law, the maximum number of strikes was thirty-nine (*"forty less one"*); but the Roman Law merely said: **"The prisoner must not die."**

The beating which Herod ordered for his uncooperative prisoner followed the Jewish tradition of **thirty-nine strokes.** Modern scientists have determined that **all known diseases fall under 39 major categories.** The Bible said it this way: *"By Whose stripes, we are healed!"*

Christ suffered for us ... Who, when He was reviled, did not revile in return; when He suffered, He did not threaten, but committed Himself to God, Who judges righteously. Jesus Himself bore our sins in His own body on the cross, that we – having died to sins – might live forever; by

Whose stripes, you were healed."
1 Peter 2:23-24; paraphrased

Thirty-nine major disease groups – thirty-nine stripes. Coincidence? I think not.

og

Actual Details of Crucifixion

[WARNING: The following factual details pertaining to execution by crucifixion may prove too graphic for small children ... or squeamish adults.]

A centurion usually served as the executioner or *carnifex servorum*. While four soldiers held the prisoner down, the centurion placed a sharp, five-inch spike into the joint between the wrist and the palm. A skillful, experienced blow sent the spike through the flesh and deep into the wood; four or five more strokes hammered the spike deeper into the rough-hewn plank, with a last blow turning it up so that the hands could not slip free.

A small projection – which resembled a rhinoceros horn, and was known as the *sedile* – fitted solidly through the crotch. This was positioned to take much of the weight off the condemned man's hands. Then a spike was driven through each foot, securing all limbs to the cross.

The wounds in the hands sent fire down through the arms. Fainting relieved only temporarily. Pain in the back, arms, hands, feet, and crotch was a dull, throbbing, horrible, endless pain. The pain built up, multiplied, was cumulative. There was not a moment of respite.

Using a series of pulleys and ropes, the crucified prison nailed on the cross was raised, and the device planted with a firm thus into a hole, positioned so the greatest amount of sunlight would pierce the prisoner's eyes. The sun shown directly into the eyes of the crucified; even when the lids were closed, a red glare penetrated.

Below, the curious waited, fascinated by the torture. The macabre scene was played out slowly. Dying should be a private thing, not a public spectacle. There was something obscene about a mob of people standing around, watching and waiting for the prisoner to die.

Then the thirst began. The lips were dry and cracked. The mouth was parched. The blood was hot. The skin was fevered. The greatest of all needs at that moment was a drop of cool water ... but water was denied. At the foot of the cross, the death squad drank, sneering in the face of the dying man, adding to his mental torment. The tongue thickened. What once was saliva was now like raw wool.

Swelling began in the hands and feet. The sedile dug deeply into unprotected genitals. It was impossible to turn, to change one's position. Muscles began to twitch. The real horror was only beginning; what had happened until now was only "child's play."

One by one, the muscles of the back gathered into tight, knotty cramps. There was no escaping them, no pulling out of them, no gentle massaging hands to ease the cramps away. The cramps moved across the shoulders and upper body, down into the abdomen. After two hours on a cross, every muscle in the body was locked in solid knots, and the agony was beyond endurance. Men shrieked themselves into insanity.

The pain and symptoms were identical to *tetanus* (lock-jaw). Man, with all his genius, has never devised a crueler or more agonizing death than that of tetanus: the slow, steady contraction of every muscle. Death by crucifixion made the agony last as long as possible.

Each hour was an eternity. At times, the cramps made the neck rigid and the head was held flush with the vertical beam. A man longed for death; it was his only remaining ambition.

There were flies and insects, the yelps of dogs with the smell of blood in their nostrils. Birds of prey, the scavengers of the skies, circled lower and lower. Prayers seemed to mock a man ... but the prisoner either prayed or cursed. On the cross, there was no end of suffering; only the manner and degree of suffering changed.

As the hours passed, the tiny blood vessels which feed the nerves were squeezed flat, and with the lack of circulation came a numbing paralysis. But a new agony developed for those who lingered on the cross: the agony of the mucous membrane.

The mucous membrane is a thin, slippery tissue which lines and lubricates much of the human body. On the cross, the mucous membrane dried to the consistency of fine gravel, and scraped the tender tissues of the posterior opening of the alimentary canal. It tore at the tortured throat. It lay like stones in the sinuses. It ripped layers of tissue from the eyes every time the pupil was moved or the eyelid blinked. Could there ever be more intense suffering this side of Hell?

If the execution squad grew bored and the prisoner still lived, soldiers were inclined to hasten death, and they began breaking bones. Standing on a ladder leaned up against the cross, a practiced legionnaire swung a mallet in a short arc, instantly shattering the right *femur* (thigh-bone). A second sharp blow shattered the left thigh. Finally, the thrust of a sword or spear between the ribs and directly into the heart would ensure death had occurred.

Be utterly convinced: **Jesus Christ did die.** He did not lapse into a deep coma, only to revive three days later. He did not freeze into suspended animation. He did not experience an "out-of-body" episode. He died completely. His bodily functions ceased, and His Spirit departed.

Most condemned men died nude. Jesus Christ was crucified. He died the most brutal death ever devised by Man. Thus was His resurrection the most complete victory over death!

ॐ

The Business of Salvation

The job description for Jesus Christ was: ***"Save the people."*** He was so filled with compassion for Mankind that He gave His whole life to redeeming us. Even as He was dying, He still had the strength to reach out to those criminals who were being crucified on either side of Him:

Two others, both criminals, were led out to be executed with Him. When they came to a place called The Skull, the [Roman soldiers] nailed Him to the cross. And the criminals were also crucified – one on His right and one on His left. Jesus said, "Father, forgive them, for they don't know what they are doing." The soldiers gambled for His clothes by throwing dice.

The crowd watched, and their leaders scoffed. "He saved others," they said, "so let Him save Himself, if He is really God's Messiah, the Chosen One."

The soldiers mocked Him too by offering Him a drink of sour wine. They called out to Him, "If You are the King of the Jews, save Yourself!" A sign was fastened above Him with these words: "This is the King of the Jews."

One of the criminals hanging beside Him scoffed, "So You're the Messiah, are You? Prove it by saving Yourself – and us too, while You're at it!"

But the other criminal protested, "Don't you fear God even when you have been sentenced to die? We deserve to die for our crimes, but this Man hasn't done anything wrong." Then he said, "Jesus, remember me when You come into Your Kingdom."

And Jesus replied, "I assure you, today you will be with Me in Paradise."
Luke 23:32-43

This second criminal – paying the final price of his sins – in his heart received an understanding of Who Jesus was. Despite his own suffering and impending death, he was able to call out to Jesus and ask for His salvation – and Jesus, with His unlimited compassion, granted him Eternal Life right there on the spot! Asking Jesus to come into our hearts, to forgive our sins and make us new, to pay our debt and restore the broken fellowship with God – this is how simply and easily salvation can be received!

The Passover Fulfilled in the Lamb of God

In fulfillment of the Feast of the Passover and Isaiah's prophecy, Jesus bore our griefs and carried our sorrows. He was wounded for our transgressions and bruised for our iniquities. The Lord God laid on Jesus the iniquity of all us. He was oppressed and afflicted. Yet He opened not His mouth, like a lamb led to the slaughter.

At three o'clock, as the people were praising God and slaughtering their Passover lambs, Jesus died. Mark was careful to note the time and wrote that it was the ninth hour (three o'clock Jewish time) when Jesus breathed His last breath (see Mark 15:33-37).

Jesus gave His total self to be roasted and consumed in the judgment fires of God as He died for our sins. The spit on which the Passover lambs were spread open was shaped like a cross-bar, which foreshadowed Jesus hanging on the cross of Calvary.

All the other details concerning the death of the Passover lambs happened to Jesus, the real Lamb of God. For example, His bones were not broken. Remember that God had said not to break any bones in the Passover lambs (see Exodus 12:46; Numbers 9:12; Psalms 34:20)? When a person is crucified, his body sags so that he cannot breathe. This causes him to push himself up with his heels just long enough to take a deep breath. To hasten the person's death, a Roman soldier would break his legs; thus he would not be ale to push himself up to get air but would suffocate.

John records that the soldiers routinely broke the legs of the two thieves who were crucified next to Jesus. But when they came to Jesus, they saw He was already dead and so did not break His legs (see John 19:31-33). When John realized this, he wrote, *"For these things were done that the Scripture should be fulfilled: 'Not one of His bones shall be broken'"* (John 19:36; also see Psalm 34:20).

The Temple Veil

History reveals that after Moses led the Hebrews out of Egypt, he was faced with the challenge of forging a nation from a bunch of slaves. God gave him the Ten Commandments, and later established a detailed form of worship involving the Tabernacle, with a serving class of priests.

The Tablets of the Ten Commandments were reverently placed within the Ark of the Covenant, which was then settled into the "Holy of Holies" – a sacred room deep within the confines of the Tabernacle, sealed and protected by a thick, woven cloth "veil." The Holy of Holies was accessible only to the High Priest, and only on one day each year: the Feast of Atonement, which was held on the tenth day of the month of Tishri.

Later, when Solomon built his glorious Temple, and later still, when the Temple was restored in Nehemiah's day, the Holy of Holies was transferred from a tent into a building. This sacred room was considered the most important place in all Israel, and its sanctity was guarded and protected by all God-fearing Jews.

The word "veil" tends to cause modern Readers to visualize a gauzy length of cloth, much like a delicate bridal veil today. But the original Temple

Veil – and all those which refurbished and re-placed it over centuries – was a heavy lock-stitch weaving that created a thick, non-opaque curtain, dense enough to deflect a hail of arrows, a powerful thrust of a sharp spear or even the slash of a penetrating sword. It was probably the first woven "armor" created – and it was hung as a continuous sheet from ceiling to floor, side-to-side; a formidable barrier. It was so weighty that it took two associate priests to lift it aside enough to permit the officiating priest to slip under and thus enter the Holy of Holies.

The impenetrable Temple Veil signified that ordinary Man could no longer have direct access to the presence of God. Since Adam sinned and was banished from the Garden of Eden, his treasured fellowship with God was distorted and heavily penalized by a complicated series of sacrifices, cleansing ceremonies and rigorous adherence to strict laws – all detailed in both the Abrahamic Covenant and through the Laws of Moses. The Temple Veil was a solid expanse of cloth through which only a devout and sanctified priest of the highest rank and of impeccable character could enter into God's presence on Earth.

The Temple Veil was the last and most closely-guarded barrier between Man and God ... and as Jesus breathed His last breath – thus completing the Ultimate Sacrifice which God demanded for the salvation of Mankind – the Hand of God Himself reached out from the Holy of Holies and ripped the Veil from top to bottom, flinging aside this heavy cloth as easily as breaking a spider's web. In this way, the only "intermediary" needed was no longer a devout and sanctified priest of the highest rank and impeccable character ... but the simple acceptance of the Final Sacrifice of the Lamb of God as our Intermediary. Thus the Holiest Room of all was opened to all who would enter by faith in Jesus Christ.

"It Is Finished"

Jesus Christ was born to die. Man's attempts to re-enter God's fellowship and presence had been continually inadequate. Yet the Father so longed for His beloved children – Mankind, of all His creation, along fashioned in His own Image – that He willingly offered the Lamb nearest to His heart ... choosing to allow His Son to suffer sorrow, horror, pain ... permitting His Heir to die in what Satan perceived as a great personal victory. When Jesus died on the cross, **never again** would God demand the shedding of anyone's or any-thing's blood as sacrifice. The work was comp-letely and forever finished. Jesus did it more than satisfactorily.

ଔ

Ten thousand angels stood by helplessly and watched legions of demons confiscate the dead soul of Jesus and carry His shattered remains down to the pits of Hell. A great wail of mourning resounded through the streets of Heaven, and

God the Father bowed His head as tears slid down His eternal face. His Son was dead.

≪ა≫

BIBLE QUIZ

(1) True or False: Jesus Christ was born to die.

True. He asked God the Father for the task.

(2) Who is the first documented person known to (literally) follow Jesus' command to *"take up My cross and follow Me"* (see Matthew 16:24, Mark 10:21)?

Simon of Cyrene, who was forcefully commanded by Roman soldiers to help Jesus carry His cross out of Jerusalem to Golgotha.

(3) Who is the first documented person known to have accepted Jesus Christ as his Savior?

The thief who asked Jesus to remember him when He comes into His Kingdom.

(4) True or False: After Jesus died on the cross, God continues to demand sacrifice.

*False. When Jesus died on the cross, **never again** would God demand the shedding of anyone's or anything's blood as sacrifice. The work was completely and forever finished; Jesus did it more than satisfactorily.*

Day 7 (Saturday)
What Was *Really* Going On?

BIBLE READING

Sad Responsibilities of Death

*Evening had already come, because it was the prepara-tion day (that is, the day before the Sabbath), Joseph of Arimathea (a prominent member of the San Hedrin Council, who had **not** consented to the plan and actions of the Council; himself was waiting for the Kingdom of God, for he was a secret disciple of Jesus) came, and he gathered up courage to go before Pilate, to ask for the Body of Jesus. Pilate wondered if He was dead by this time, and summoning the centurion, he questioned him as to whether He was already dead. Then ascertaining this from the centurion, he granted the Body to Joseph.*

Joseph bought a linen cloth, took Him down from the cross, and wrapped Him in the linen cloth. And Nicodemus came also (who had first come to Him by night), bringing a mixture of myrrh and aloes, about a hundred pounds of weight. So they took the Body of Jesus, and bound it in linen wrappings with the spices, as is the burial custom of the Jews.

Now near the place where He was crucified, there was a garden; and in the garden, a new tomb (in which no one had yet been laid; it was intended for Joseph of Arimathea's personal use), cut out of the rock. Therefore, on account of the Jewish day of preparation and because the tomb was nearby, Joseph and Nicodemus laid Jesus there, and rolled a stone against the entrance of the tomb. And Mary Magdalene and Mary the Mother of Jesus were looking on, to see where He was laid.

Schemers Still At Large

Now on the next day (which is the one after the preparation), the chief priests and the Pharisees gathered together with Pilate and said, "Sir, we remember that when He was still alive, that deceiver said, 'After three days, I am to rise again.'

"Therefore, give orders for the grave to be made secure until the third day, lest the disciples come and steal Him away, and say to the people, 'He has risen from the dead,' for the last deception will be worse than the first."

Pilate answered, "You have a guard; go, make it as secure as you know how." And they went and made the grave secure; and along with the guard, they set a seal on the stone.

And the disciples and all the followers of Jesus – fearing further reprisals from the San Hedrin, and perhaps arrest from the Romans – went into hiding, where they wept and mourned the death of Jesus.

A Blend of All Four Gospels; paraphrased

BIBLE STUDY

If Only the Walls Could Speak!

When Jesus Christ was arrested and under-went hours of terrible physical abuse, mental and emotional torture, and eventually an inhuman death, His disciples immediately went into hiding. With the exception of His Mother, Mary Magdalene and John the Beloved, the fact is that His most trusted companions – those to whom He had entrusted the Kingdom of God – scurried out of sight just as quickly as they could. First to run to save his neck was, of course, Peter – so-called "the Rock" – whose denial of Christ had begun even before His death.

What a dismal scene that Upper Room must have witnessed! Where a few hours before the Son of God had feasted His friends and spoke to them powerful words of encouragement – even prophesying His death and specifically foretelling His resurrection – now the Upper Room was filled with sobs and wails as the followers of Jesus contemplated the (apparent) destruction of their hopes and dreams, the seemingly dismal failure of His grand plans to bring about the Kingdom of God on Earth.

Also they feared further attacks by the San Hedrin, attacks in which they might be forced to pay the ultimate price. Perhaps even the Romans might be looking for Jesus' followers, to question them and possibly imprison them for any alleged association with insurrection and treason. The fear of the unknown suffocated them.

Therefore, it fell to two remarkable men – Joseph of Arimathea and Nicodemus – and two remarkable women – Mary Magdalene and Mary the Mother of Jesus – to deal with the broken Body of Jesus (and although he is not mentioned in the Bible at this stage, it is assumed that John the Beloved was helping the broken-hearted women). Each of these persons had distinctly different motives for taking the risk of exposing themselves.

Mixed Motives

The Bible clearly tells us that Joseph of Arimathea was not only a rich man, but also a respected member of the San Hedrin ... and a secret disciple of Jesus. (To be eligible for a seat on the San Hedrin, Joseph must have fulfilled several stringent requirements; among them, his venerable age, his intelligent knowledge of the Scriptures, his powers of reasoning, and his sense of justice.) He had been voted down in the debate and trial of Jesus (contrary to some reports, it was **not** a unanimous decision by the San Hedrin to crucify Jesus), and had probably stormed out of the Council chambers, repudiating their vindictive and false decision to have Him killed.

Joseph of Arimathea's motive? He wants to right a wrong, if possible, in any way he could contribute. He exhibited *fileo* – the love of a brother.

Nicodemus, on the other hand, was a young and wealthy man, and his personal encounters with Jesus had left him with many questions and much dissatisfaction of heart. He was probably too young yet to be considered for a seat on the San Hedrin, but he was certainly of the class which ascended to positions of political power and public recognition.

Nicodemus' motive? He want to prove at last His understanding and acceptance of Jesus as the Messiah. He experiences *agape* – love divinely imparted by God

Mary Magdalene was already a notoriously emotional person. Her outbursts of devotion to Jesus did little to endear her to all of the disciples, yet He praised her above many others for her sensitivity. She had unknowingly already begun burial preparations for Jesus even before His death (see Matthew 26:7), and it was completely natural for her to stand at the foot of the cross until the bitter end, and to be there to help with the final arrangements.

Mary Magdalene's motive? She loved Him, even in death. Her heart was utterly committed to the Man, Jesus of Nazareth. She exhibited **eros** – the natural (although not enacted), wholesome human love of a woman for a man.

Lastly, Mary the Mother of Jesus was there. She of all people had the right to tend to her Son's body. Personally, I love the tender marble depiction by the great artist Michelangelo, which is called "the *Pieta*," meaning "the sorrow." It portrays a gracious woman sitting down, the limp form of her Son draped across her lap. Not a Madonna and Child, but an older woman with a crucified Son. Doctors today tell us one of the worst griefs to hit humankind is the death of a child.

Mary the Mother's motive? He was her Son. She had given birth to Him, she had cared for Him in His infancy and childhood ... now she would bury Him. She exhibited **familia** – the love and duty of a parent for a child.

Aftermath of Sorrow

So it was that the remaining eleven disciples (Judas Iscariot had long since cut himself off from the group, and – unknown to them at the time – had already committed suicide by hanging) huddled in the Upper Room, which was a refuge for them ... and the probably origin of the underground Church. It is postulated that the Upper Room was located in some building belonging to Joseph of Arimathea, possibly his own residence.

There was no victory song sung this day ... no delight of hearing God's Word preached ... no shouts of joy when signs and wonders were made known ... no sense of purpose to be fulfilled. The Light of the World had been extinguished. If anything, a funeral dirge would have mournfully sounded.

By this time, the Romans were quite disgusted with the whole mess. Since Pilate – whose Roman religious beliefs did not extend to the possibility of life after death – had ascertained from the testimony of the death squad's centurion, that Jesus was indeed dead, he sourly granted permission for the San Hedrin to mount a guard and seal the tomb where the Body of that "unfortunate" Prophet was interred. He had already washed his hands of the whole affair, and really wanted nothing further to do with it.

History of the Blood

The true images and sounds of the Season of the Lamb: the cruel crown of thorns ... a rough-hewn wooden cross ... a mocking, jeering mob ... nail-spiked hands and feet ... the ravaged form of the Savior hanging limply ... wails of anguish from His Mother and disciples ... an unnaturally storm-darkened sky. The most important element of that terrible crucifixion day was the massive loss of Jesus' life-blood.

The significance of blood goes right back to the Book of Genesis. When Cain and Abel – the firstborn sons of Adam and Eve – initially brought their sacrifices to honor God, even then God had **already ordained** that only the ending of a life and the shedding of blood would suffice. **A sacrifice which costs little is worth little.**

Cain had brought the best of his harvest yield: golden sheaves of grain, ripened boughs of fruit, succulent clusters of earth-grown produce. With pride in himself and his accomplishments, he piled his sacrifice on the altar and lit it afire, lazily watching the smoke rise up to Heaven, fully expecting God to receive his offering.

As he waited for God's response, he glanced around on the fields, gardens and orchards stretching abundantly around him, and saw there was much more bounty to be had. He knew this token of sacrifice would not deplete his resources. God saw into Cain's heart and knew his motivation ... and rejected his offering primarily because it did not include the requisite of shed blood. Cain became angry, saying, "God, You are not fair!"

Abel had brought the fairest of his flocks: a spotless young lamb, his personal favorite, a beloved pet. He lovingly cradled the lamb in his arms, spoke gently into its curly-coated ear of the sweet affection and joy he had enjoyed with this innocent creature. Then, obediently, Abel tenderly laid the lamb onto the kindling, and – weeping unashamedly – swiftly plunged a knife into its throat, pouring out its blood and eventually severing its life.

He watched as the spark of life faded from his beloved pet's eyes, then turned his tear-stained face toward Heaven and said to God, "This is my best gift." As the fragrant smoke from this altar rose toward Heaven, God saw deep into Abel's heart ... and accepted His offering.

Blood Is Life

Blood is the conduit of Life. Our bodies – and this is true for most of Creation, as we know it – depend on the circulation of blood for survival. Blood regulates temperature, and carries nutrients, oxygen, waste products, antibodies – from one part of the body to another, which is necessary for existence. The average adult has about ten pints (4.7 liters) of blood in his system; the heart pumps all ten pints every minute when the body is at rest.

Blood is Life, and the deliberate loss of blood will cause Life to cease. If an important blood vessel – such as the femoral artery or the carotid artery – is punctured or severed, and the flow of blood is not immediately staunched, it would take less than ten minutes for the average adult to bleed to death and die.

Through the cruel punishment of crucifixion – where the Body of Jesus was impaled and torn open (in His hands and feet, around His head from the crown of thorns, and all the places the whip-lashes had landed) – He slowly and painfully bled to death. Later, when the Roman soldiers stabbed Him in the side to be certain He was truly dead, only pale blood-tinged water (which is indicative of failed cardiac function) flowed out ... because Jesus had already poured out **ALL** His life's Blood. Jesus offered up His very own Blood in sacrifice to His Father as payment for **our sin.**

The Blood of Jesus has tremendous proper-ties, and He has made it available to us today.

When Satan saw the Blood of Jesus seeping from the wounds on His flogged back, from the gouges dug into His face and head by the thorns, from the holes spiked into His hands and feet – the Evil One laughed with glee to see the most critical aspect of His Life draining from the Son's Body. What he did not recognize **then** was that by freely giving away His Blood, Jesus was actually empowering **us** with His very Life. That flow of Blood spelled doom for Satan ... and he did not realize it at the time.

Today Satan Fears the Blood of Jesus

The Blood of Jesus gives us power to over-come Satan and all his evil works:

(1) We are **redeemed** by the Blood –

You were not redeemed with corruptible things, like silver or gold, but with the precious Blood of Christ, as of a lamb without blemish and without spot.

1 Peter 1:18-19

Christ's sacrificial death paid the price to ransom us from the bondage to sin, death and Satan.

(2) We are **justified** by the Blood –

Much more then, having now been justified by His Blood, we shall be saved from wrath through Him.

Romans 5:9

Because of the shed Blood of Christ, assigned to the sinner and received by faith (see Romans 3:25), God declares us to be righteous by His sight, and releases us from the guilt and penalty of sin.

(3) We are **sanctified** by the Blood –

Jesus also, that He might sanctify the people with His own Blood, suffered outside the gate.

Hebrews 13:12

Like the scapegoat on the Day of Atonement (see Leviticus 16), Jesus suffered outside Jerusalem's gate – on the hill of Golgotha – to remove our sins from us.

(4) We are **cleansed** by the Blood –

If we walk in the light as God is in the light, the Blood of Jesus Christ, His Son, cleanses us from all sin.

1 John 1:7

When we walk obediently in the light of God's will, Christ's Blood provides continuous cleansing for our sins.

(5) We are **reconciled** by the Blood –

It pleased the Father to reconcile all things to Himself by Christ, whether things on Earth or things in Heaven, having made peace through the Blood of His Cross. And you, who once were alienated and enemies in your minds by wicked works, yet now He has reconciled in the Body of His Flesh through death, to present you holy and blameless and above reproach in His sight.

Colossians 1:20-22

In our sinful condition, humanity is alienated from God; but through the sacrifice of Christ, we are restored to a right relationship with our Creator.

(6) We have **access to God** through the Blood –

Now in Christ Jesus you, who once were far off, have been made near by the Blood of Christ.

Ephesians 2:13

We can enter boldly and confidently into the very presence of God *"by the Blood of Jesus, by a new and living way which He consecrated for us"* (Hebrews 10:20).

(7) We have **an eternal covenant** sealed in Christ's Blood –

May the God of peace, Who brought up our Lord Jesus from the dead, through the Blood of the everlasting covenant, make you complete in every good work.

Hebrews 13:20-21

The covenant God made with the Hebrews was ratified when the people were sprinkled with the blood of sacrificial animals (see Exodus 24). The New Covenant is ratified with the shed Blood of Jesus Christ, *"the Mediator of a better covenant"* (see Hebrews 8:6). Christ's Blood is the seal on the blessings of the New Covenant: pardon, peace, provision, protection, the presence of the Holy Spirit, and much more.

There's Power In the Blood

Would you be free from the burden of sin?

There's power in the Blood, power in the Blood
Would you o'er evil a victory win?
There's wonderful power in the Blood

There is power, power, wonder-working power
In the Blood of the Lamb
There is power, power, wonder-working power
In the precious Blood of the Lamb!

Would you be free from your passion and pride?
There's power in the Blood, power in the Blood
Come for a cleansing to Calvary's tide
There's wonderful power in the Blood

Would you be whiter, much whiter than snow?
There's power in the Blood, power in the Blood
Sin-stains are lost in its life-giving flow
There's wonderful power in the Blood

Would you do service for Jesus your King?
There's power in the Blood, power in the Blood
Would you live daily His praises to sing?
There's wonderful power in the Blood.

– Lewis E. Jones

ⱷ

[**WARNING**: Once again, this **fictional** short story may be too graphic for young children or squeamish adults to assimilate; please use parental discretion and wisdom.]

DOWN TO THE PIT

The volume of noise was incredible. Howls of demons – chanting in exultation, screaming their approval to their victorious master, cheering, taunting, hideous laughter – was heard long before anyone (or anything) entered the vacant throne room. A terrible roar filled the murky chamber like a wild, stormy ocean, battering the senses and pebbling chills.

Then, an entire wall burst apart in a shower of sparks and rubble as one mighty, clawed foot thrust in with explosive force. Dozens of scamp-ering imps spilled into the chamber, dancing around with insane pleasure, beckoning their master through the hole. Satan entered, carrying the lifeless body of Jesus across his shoulders in cruel mockery of the manner in which devout Jews carried lambs to the Temple for sacrifice.

To the furious accolades of his fiendish minions, he circled a giant conference table again and again, flaunting his prize. Then, laughing uproariously, Satan flung the unresisting corpse onto the slab-like table, where it rolled to a limp, wooden halt.

From beneath the ghastly throne at the end of the room, inside a cage built of rusted iron bars, thousands of frightened, horrified eyes stared at the scene. These people of God who had died throughout the ages – partakers of the Old Covenant, now imprisoned in Satan's stronghold – gaped numbly at the remains of God's own Son, lying limply, lifelessly, powerlessly in front of them. All hope was lost.

A great wail rose from within the prison. As he marched toward his throne, Satan snarled victoriously at the captives, who shrunk back in renewed fear. Then he seated himself above them with malicious dignity, and watched as his demon-lords poked and abused the battered dead body of his most-hated enemy, enjoying their reviling. They had wrapped heavy chains – their own symbols of death – around the body, binding it grotesquely, weighting it down and diminishing it until it seemed to flatten and sink into the table-top.

Satan Presents Awards

Finally raising his hand for attention, gradually the din subsided, and Satan gazed at his demons simpering before him. Singling out Murder, he beckoned and the beast lumbered forward to kneel before his master. "Murder, my dishonorable servant, I must congratulate you on an outstandingly diabolic performance today. You have delivered into my power He Who has eluded me for so long! I … have … won!" He threw his head back and laughed.

A tremendous cheer resounded, and more demons jumped up to dance in grisly celebration. Satan raised his hand again. "And Hatred, you nasty old fellow," the talon pointed at another demon-master. "I am so pleased with your vile accomplishments. I believe I shall let you continue reproducing yourself throughout the whole Earth as your reward." Shrill giggles of glee greeted this unexpected favor.

"And as for you, Fear, my own name-sake …" But before Satan could continue, a sonic boom of indefinable sound burst upon the audio devices of the assembly, and demons clamped whatever appendages they owned over whatever orifices they had to protect themselves. A brilliant, piercing light suddenly flooded the gruesome chamber, and demons cringed beneath the conference table, cowering with fear and surprise. "What …?" croaked Satan, stunned.

The Whirlwind of God

Then a new wind began. With a shout that strangely resembled music, a whirlwind swept into the chamber and whipped furiously at everyone and everything. The blood-soaked hair on the head of the victim stirred with the blast, giving a haunting animation to the corpse, which now trembled in the storm. Satan stood stock-still, frozen, his fanged mouth hanging open.

Just as suddenly as it had begun, the wind ceased. A long pause filled the chamber, with only the distant crackling of Hell's eternal flames disturbing the silence. And just as frightened demons started to poke their misshapen heads out of hiding, a deep rumbling Voice resounded:

"THIS is My beloved Son, in Whom I AM VERY well pleased."

As the rumble of that Voice slowly echoed and faded, a close darkness filled the chamber and the very sulphur-laden air was swept out. The sweetest, purest of breezes began to pour into the black-lightless chamber … and the body of Jesus began to sparkle and glow with unearthly illumination – so like the light of … Creation. First to grasp the significance of what was happening before his eyes, Satan managed to gasp, "No!"

The soft breeze caressed the broken body, stroking Him from head to toe, and rapidly-brightening sparkles of light swirled around from fingertip to fingertip. Gently, with unceasing care and eternal patience, the wind and the light infused themselves into the corpse … and He began to quiver ever so slightly. Those who had witnessed the Creation of Adam were hauntingly reminded of that miracle now.

Heedless of possible danger to himself, Satan sprang forward and tried to grab the body … only to be repelled by an unseen force which now completely cocooned Jesus. "He's mine!" Satan bellowed. "He's dead! I have won! You cannot have Him!"

Abruptly, an angel stood calmly in the chamber … and a few demon hands reached for their swords and spears. He merely raised one hand, and weapons clattered everywhere. The angel pronounced, "Oh no, Lucifer, once the lovely prince of Heaven. You have not won at all." He spoke conversationally. "This –" a slender hand pointed at the rapidly stirring body – "**is** the Lamb of God, Who has fulfilled **all** the Father's requirements, He Who has willingly sacrificed His very own life for all of Mankind, He Who has given Himself as an offering for sin … He Who takes away the sin of the world forever."

"No, no, no!" Satan screeched, subsiding into a whimper. "But I ... killed ... Him." His hands covering his face, Satan wept in agony.

The angel smiled radiantly. "But God has raised Him up! Look!" Unable to look away, all present – from Satan staggering in shock, to demons frozen with amazement, to captives straining incredulously around the bars beneath the throne – watched as the Son of God's incandescent body began to tremble and move. His chest rose and fell with breath. His hands braced themselves on the table, and His arms began to raise the torso from which rips and bruises were rapidly fading. His eyelids fluttered, then snapped open, and a huge smile spread across His face. Undeniably murdered by the most thorough and gruesome means of death, now Jesus Christ was alive!

Re-Creation

Within a blink, the battered, bloodless body was restored to perfect, vibrant wholeness. A bloom of health and joy flushed His warm cheeks to a husky color. With the exception of piercings still seen on His hands and feet and a spear-mark on His side, all evidence of torture, death and decay were gone, and a vigorous Man of 33 human-years once again stood tall and strong.

The angel reverently approached and kneeled, offering Him a shimmering white robe, which He took and swept over His nudity, clothing Himself in Glory. Unable to suppress a grin, the angel winked … and vanished.

Satan sank to his knees, trembling. Jesus gazed at His oldest enemy. "Lucifer, my once-friend, look at Me."

Agony contorting his face, Satan dared not disobey. *"How are you fallen from heaven, O star of the morning, son of the dawn?"* Jesus quoted from the writings of the prophet Isaiah. "You have been cut down to the Earth, you who have weakened the nations. For you said in your heart, *'I will ascend to Heaven; I will raise my throne above the stars of God; and I will sit on the mount of assembly in the recesses of the north. I will ascend above the heights of the clouds; I will make myself like the Most High.'* Tsk, tsk, tsk."

Jesus raised a bare, nail-scarred foot and brought it down on Satan's head, forcing his ashen face to the floor. "You wicked dragon! For this you have been thrust down to Sheol, to the recesses of the pit. Those who see you will gaze at you and will ponder over you, saying, *'Is this he who made the Earth tremble, who shook kingdoms, who made the world like a wilderness and overthrew cities, who did not allow his prisoners to go home?'* You are despised and rejected in Heaven and in Earth. You … are … **defeated!'**

Jesus Reveals the Lamb

"But, Holy Prince, Precious Son, um, Jesus Messiah …" Satan began to beg, his lips smashed against the floor, "… I did not know …"

"You have **always** known, My old enemy," Jesus retorted, "if you had only bothered to properly look. I have indeed fulfilled every requirement which My Father set before Me – and it was all prophesied years ago. The Father required a perfect lamb – **I am that Perfect Lamb.** The Father required a blood sacrifice – **I have poured out all of My Blood.** The Father required an atonement for sin – I have taken your first plan of destruction, even from the day of Adam and Eve, and **have erased all the effects of sin for all Mankind,** for all who will receive Me.

Jesus Passes Sentence

"And as for you, you filthy serpent, remember this (for you will hear it again later):

There was a war in Heaven. Michael and his angels waged war with the dragon, who waged war with his angels. But they were not strong enough, and there was no longer a place found for them in Heaven. So the great dragon was thrown down, the serpent of old that is called Satan, who deceives the whole world; he was thrown down to the Earth, and his angels were thrown down with him.

"Then there will be a loud voice in Heaven, saying, 'Now the salvation, and the power, and the Kingdom of our God and the authority of His Christ have come, for the accuser of our brothers has been thrown down, who accuses them before our God day and night. And they overcame him because of the Blood of the Lamb and because of the word of their testimony; and they did not love their life even to death. For this reason, rejoice, O Heavens and you who dwell in them. Woe to the Earth and the sea, because the devil has come down to you, having great wrath, knowing that he has only a short time.'"

As Satan thrashed beneath Christ's firmly-planted foot, Jesus continued:

"For I see an angel coming down from Heaven, having a key of the abyss and a

great chain in his hand. He will lay hold of the dragon, the serpent of old, who is Satan, and will bind him for a thousand years, and throw him into the abyss and shut and seal it over him, so that he should not deceive the nations any longer, until the thousand years are accomplished."

All the citizens of Hell burst out with cries of anguish at this terrible sentence of doom. Then Jesus concluded:

"And when the thousand years are complete, Satan will be released from his prison, and will come out to deceive the nations. There shall be a war, and they shall come upon the broad plain of the Earth and around the ramp of the saints and the beloved city. Then fire shall come down from Heaven and devour them. And the devil who deceived them will be thrown into the Lake of Fire and Brimstone, and will be tormented day and night forever and ever.

"Then shall we see a Great White Throne and Him Who sits upon it, from Whose presence Earth and Heaven flee away. And all the dead – the great and the small – shall stand before the Throne, and the

Book of Life shall be opened and the dead shall be judged from the things which are written therein, according to their deeds. And if anyone's name is not found written in the Book of Life, he shall be thrown into the Lake of Fire."

Jesus paused, and moved His foot a little. Satan fearfully raised his head a little, groveling. Jesus commanded: "Now … give Me your keys."

Satan's eyes opened wider with renewed shock, and his hands fumbled to clutch the great iron ring belted to his waist. "My keys …?" he stammered.

"Give Me the keys to Death, to Hell, to the grave. I have overcome you once and for all, and you are doomed to eternal damnation." Jesus lowered His foot once more on Satan's head, and the creature howled in agony and despair. Jesus declared, "I am the First and the Last. I am the Living One; I was dead, and behold, I am alive forevermore! My work on Earth is accomplished" – Jesus reached down and snatched the entire ring of keys from Satan – "and **now I have the keys!"**

With a roar, the doors which had caged the people of the Old Covenant burst open, and thousands of rejoicing saints rushed out. Surrounding their Savior, they hoisted Him up on their shoulders and joyously carried Him through the blown-out wall, trampling on cowering demons. As He vanished from their view, Jesus called back to the crushed remnants of Satan and his followers, "You had better practice riding that Pale Horse of yours, because I am coming back again!"

BIBLE QUIZ

(1) True or False: After Jesus died, the Pharisees were satisfied, and let His disciples go free.

False. Not only did they persist in harassing Jesus' disciples, but they continued to fear Jesus Himself. Even in death, they feared His ongoing influence.

(2) Why did God accept Abel's sacrifice but not Cain's?

Abel's sacrifice was of a gift which meant a great deal to him, and included the death and shedding of blood; Cain's sacrifice was out of his lavish wealth, little more than a "tip" to God, and it did not include the required shedding of blood.

(3) Which disciples buried Jesus' body?

Joseph of Arimathea and Nicodemus – although not counted among the original twelve chosen disciples – accompanied Mary His Mother, the "other" Mary (usually designated

"Magdalene") and John the Beloved, when they took down His body, quickly cleaned it (because the Sabbath was approaching and time was short) and then laid it in Joseph of Arimathea's own tomb.

(4) **Memorize:**

It pleased the Father to reconcile all things to Himself by Christ, whether things on Earth or things in Heaven, having made peace through the Blood of His Cross.   And you, who once were alienated and enemies in your minds by wicked works, yet now He has reconciled in the Body of His Flesh through death, to present you holy and blameless and above reproach in His sight.

Colossians 1:20-22

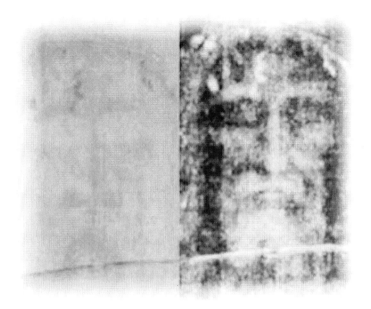

Day 8 (Lamb's Sunday)
Alive Forevermore

BIBLE READING

Early in the Morning

When the Sabbath was over, the women – Mary Magdalene, Mary (the mother of James), Salome, and Joanna – brought spices, that they might come and anoint Jesus. Very early on the first day of the week, they came to the tomb when the sun had risen. As they were entering the garden, they said to one another, "Who will roll away the stone for us from the entrance of the tomb?" But when they arrived at the tomb, they saw that the stone had already been rolled away, although it was extremely large.

(A severe earthquake had occurred, for an angel of the Lord had descended from Heaven, and came and rolled away the stone, and now sat upon it. His appearance was like lightning, and his garment was as white as snow. The guards shook for fear of him, and fainted like dead men.)

Then, entering the tomb, they saw a young man sitting at the right, wearing a white robe, and they were amazed. The women were terrified, and bowed their faces to the ground. He said to them, "Do not be amazed. You are looking for Jesus the Nazarene, Who has been crucified, aren't you? He has risen, He is not here. Remember how He spoke to you while He was still in Galilee, saying that the Son of Man must be delivered into the hands of sinful men, be crucified, and the third day rise again?"

And they remembered His words. The angel continued, "Behold, here is the place where they laid Him. Now go, tell His disciples and Peter: 'He is going before you into Galilee; there you will see Him, just as He said to you'."

Then the women fled from the tomb, for trembling and astonishment (and great joy) had gripped them, and they said nothing to anyone, for they were afraid.

Simon Peter and John the Beloved Investigate

After He had risen early on the first day of the week, Mary Magdalene reported to those who had been with Him, while they were mourning and weeping; she reported, "They have taken away the Lord out of the tomb, and we do not know where they have laid Him." Simon Peter and John the Beloved arose and ran to the tomb together. John arrived first, and he stooped and looked in, seeing the linen wrapping lying there (but he did not go in).

Then Simon Peter arrived at the tomb, and he entered it. He beheld the linen wrapping lying there. He saw the face-cloth which had been on His head, which was not lying with the linen wrappings but was rolled up in a place by itself. Then John entered the tomb as well, and together they saw and believed. However, they did not understand the Scripture (that He must first rise again from the dead), so they went away.

Mary Magdalene and "the Gardener"

But Mary stood outside the tomb, weeping. Then she stooped and looked inside the tomb, where she saw two angels in white, sitting (one at the head, and one at the feet, where the Body of Jesus had been lying). The angels asked her, "Woman, why are you weeping?"

Mary answered, "Because they have taken away my Lord, and I do not know where they have laid Him." Then she turned around and saw Jesus standing there; but she did not recognize Him.

Jesus asked her, "Woman, why are you weeping? Whom are you seeking?"

Supposing Him to be the gardener, she pleaded, "Sir, if you have carried Him away, tell me where you have laid Him and I will take Him away!"

Then Jesus said, "Mary!"

She turned and cried, "Rabboni *(beloved Teacher)!*"

Jesus said, "Stop clinging to Me, for I have not ascended to the Father. Now go to My brothers and say to them, 'I ascend to My Father and your Father, and to My God and your God'."

Mary then went and announced to the disciples, "I have seen the Lord," and many other things that He said to her.

Miraculous Reality Battles Malicious Dishonesty

Some of the guard came into the city and reported to the chief priests all that had happened. When they had assembled with the elders and counseled together, they gave a large sum of money to the soldiers, saying, "You are to say, 'His disciples came by night and stole Him away while we were asleep.' If this should come to the governor's ears, we will win him over, and keep you out of trouble."

So they took the money and did as they had been instructed; and this story was widely spread among the Jews, and is to this day.

In Disguise On the Road to Emmaus

Two of Jesus' followers – Simon and Cleopas – were going that very day to a village named Emmaus, which was about seven miles from Jerusalem. They were conversing with each other about all these things which had taken place. While they were discussing, Jesus Himself approached and began traveling with them (but their eyes were prevented from recognizing Him). He asked, "What are these words that *you are exchanging with one another as you are walking? But they stood still, looking sad.*

Then Cleopas answered, "Are You the only One visiting Jerusalem and unaware of the things which have happened here in these days?"

Jesus replied, "What things?

They explained, "The things about Jesus the Nazarene, Who was a great Prophet, mighty in deed and word in the sight of God and all the people. Do You not know how the chief priests and our rulers delivered Him up to the sentence of death, and crucified Him? We were hoping that it was He Who was going to redeem Israel.

"Indeed, besides all this, it is the third day since these things happened. But also some women among us have amazed us, for when they were at the tomb early this morning, they did not find His Body. Then they came and said that they had also seen a vision of angels, who said that He was alive. Some of those who were with us went to the tomb and found it just exactly as the women also had said; but Him they did not see."

Then Jesus responded, "Oh foolish men and slow of heart to believe in all that the prophets have spoken! Was it not necessary for the Christ to suffer these things and to enter into His glory?" Beginning with Moses and with all the prophets, He explained to them the things concerning Himself in all the Scriptures.

As they approached the village where they were going, He indicated He would go farther. But they urged Him, "Stay with us, for it is getting toward evening and the day is nearly over." So He went in to stay with them.

That night, when He sat at the table with them, He took the bread and blessed it. Breaking it, He began giving it to them. Then their eyes were opened and they recognized Him.

Instantly, He vanished from their sight. Then they said to one another, "Were not our hearts burning within us while He was speaking to us on the road, while He was explaining the Scriptures to us?" And they rose that very hour and returned to Jerusalem.

There they found gathered together the eleven disciples and others, and reported, "The Lord has really risen!" They began to relate their experiences on the road and how He finally was recognized by them in the breaking of the bread.

Jesus "Proves" Himself to the Disciples

While Simon and Cleopas were telling these things, Jesus Himself stood in their midst. They were startled and frightened, thinking they were seeing a spirit. He reprimanded them for their unbelief and hardness of heart, because they had not believed those who had seen Him after He had risen. "Why are you troubled and why do doubts arise in your hearts? See My hands and My feet, that it is I, Myself! Touch Me and see, for a spirit does not have flesh and bones as you see that I have."

When He had said these things, He showed them His hands and feet. While they still could not believe it for joy and were marveling, He asked, "Have you anything here to eat?"

So they gave Him a piece of broiled fish. He took it and ate it before them.

Thomas Has Trouble Believing

But Thomas (called Didymus, one of the original Twelve disciples) was not with them when Jesus came, so the other disciples told him that Jesus was alive and had appeared to them. But Thomas retorted, "Unless I shall see in His hands the imprint of the nails, and put my finger into the place of the nails and put my hand into His side, I will not believe."

Eight days later, His disciples were again inside (this time, Thomas was with them). Jesus suddenly appeared (although the doors were shut) and stood in their midst, saying, "Peace be with you." Then He said to Thomas, "Reach here your finger and see My hands, and reach here your hand and put it into My side, and be not unbelieving but believing."

Thomas gasped, "My Lord and my God!"

Jesus replied,"Because you have seen Me, have you believed? Blessed are they who did not see and yet be-lieved." Many other signs therefore Jesus also performed in the presence of the disciples (which are not written in this Book), but these have been written that you may believe that Jesus is the Christ, the Son of God; and that believing, you may have life in His Name.

Breakfast On the Beach

After these things, Jesus manifested Himself again to the disciples at the Sea of Tiberias. Simon Peter, Thomas

Didymus, Nathanael of Cana, James and John (the sons of Zebedee), and two other disciples were there. Simon Peter said, "I am going fishing." They all went out in a boat, but that night they caught nothing.

When the day was breaking, Jesus stood on the beach (but the disciples did not recognize Him). He called, "Children, you do not have any fish, do you?"

They answered, "No."

Then Jesus instructed, "Cast the net on the right-hand side of the boat, and you will find a catch." They cast therefore, and then they were not able to haul it in because of the great number of fish.

John the Beloved realized, "It is the Lord!" When Simon Peter heard that, he put his outer garment on (he was stripped for work) and threw himself into the sea. The other disciples brought in the little boat (they were not far from the land, about one hundred yards away), dragging the net full of fish.

When they got out upon the land, they saw a charcoal fire already laid, and a fish placed on it, with bread. Jesus instructed, "Bring some of the fish which you have now caught." Simon Peter helped draw the net to land (the net was full of 153 fish, and although there were so many, the net was not torn). Jesus said, "Come and have breakfast." None of the disciples ventured to question Him, knowing He was the Lord.

Jesus took the bread and gave it to them, and likewise the fish. This was the third time that Jesus was manifested to the disciples after He was raised from the dead.

Jesus Restores Simon Peter

After they finished breakfast, Jesus asked Simon Peter, "Simon Peter, son of John, do you love Me more than these?"

Simon Peter answered, "Yes, Lord, You know that I love You."

Jesus said, "Tend My lambs." Then a second time, He asked, "Simon Peter, son of John, do you love Me?"

Again Simon Peter answered, "Yes, Lord, You know that I love You!"

Jesus said, "Shepherd My sheep." Then a third time, Jesus asked, "Simon Peter, son of John, do you love Me?"

Simon Peter was grieved, and he insisted, "Lord, You know all things. You know that I love You!"

And Jesus answered, "Tend My sheep. Truly I say to you, when you were younger, you used to walk wherever you wished; but when you grow old, you will stretch out your hands and someone else will bring you where you do not wish to go."

Other Appearances and Instructions

Then He said to them, "These are My words which I spoke to you while I was still with you, that all things which are written about Me in the Law of Moses and the Prophets and the Psalms must be fulfilled." And He opened their minds to understand the Scriptures. He taught them, "Thus it is written, that the Christ should suffer and rise again from the dead the third day, and that the repentance for forgiveness of sins should be proclaimed in His Name to all the nations, beginning from Jerusalem. You are witnesses of these things. Behold, I am sending forth the promise of My Father upon you. But you are to stay in the city until you are clothed with power from on high."

Jesus Mandates the Disciples

Jesus spoke to them, "All authority has been given to Me in Heaven and on Earth. Go, therefore, and make disciples of all the nations, baptizing them in the Name of the Father and the Son and the Holy Spirit; teaching them to observe all that I commanded you; and remember, I am with you always, even to the end of the age.

"Go into all the world and preach the Gospel to all creation. He who has believed and has been baptized shall be saved; but he who has disbelieved shall be condemned. And these signs will accompany those who have believed: in My Name, they will cast out demons; they will speak with new tongues; they will pick up serpents; and if they drink any deadly poison, it shall not hurt them; they will lay hands on the sick, and they will recover."

After His suffering, Jesus presented Himself alive by many convincing proofs, appearing to them over a period of forty days, speaking of the things concerning the Kingdom of God. Gathering them together, He commanded them to not leave Jerusalem but to wait for: "What the Father has promised, which you have heard of from Me. For John baptized with water, but you shall be baptized with the Holy Spirit not many days from now."

The disciples asked, "Lord, is it at this time You are restoring the Kingdom of Israel?"

Jesus answered, "It is not for you to know times or epochs which the Father has fixed by His own authority. But you shall receive power when the Holy Spirit has come upon you, and you shall be My witnesses, in Jerusalem, and in all Judea and Samaria, and even to the remotest part of the Earth."

"A Great Cloud of Witnesses ..."

He led them out as far as Bethany, and He lifted up His hands and blessed them. While He was blessing them, He parted from them. While they were looking on, a cloud received Him out of their sight. He was received up into Heaven, and sat down at the right hand of God.

While they were gazing intently into the sky, behold, two men in white clothing stood beside them and asked, "Men of Galilee, why do you stand looking into the sky? This Jesus Who has been taken up from you into Heaven will come in just the same way as you have watched Him go into Heaven."

Then they returned to Jerusalem with great joy, and were continually in the Temple, praising God. They went out and preached everywhere, while the Lord worked with them and confirmed the word by the signs that followed.

A Blend of All Four Gospels and Acts 1

BIBLE STUDY

Crushed Expectations

Have you ever thought about the tremendous sorrow, confusion and disappointment which the disciples must have felt after Jesus' death? For three years they had followed a Man Whom they understood was the holy Son of Man – Who had demonstrated great signs and wonders ... Who had taught radical new truths ... Who had promised the Kingdom of God on Earth in their lifetime – and now He was indisputably dead.

That reminds me of Charles Dickens' great opening to his famous morality tale, *"A Christmas Carol"*:

> *Marley was dead, to begin with. There is no doubt whatever about that ... Old Marley was as dead as a door-nail. ... This must be distinctly understood, or nothing wonderful can come of the story I am going to relate.*

Jesus Christ too was *"dead as a door-nail,"* and therefore, His resurrection from the dead was truly miraculous.

In several different ways, the disciples were crushed. Personally: their beloved Friend had been unjustly arrested ... unfairly prosecuted ... undeservedly sentenced ... maliciously mocked ... sadistically beaten ... and cruelly executed.

Politically: the fledgling reformation of their conquered nation – engendered by the allegedly revolutionary teachings of Jesus – was now just as dead as He was. Economically: they had all abandoned their various careers to follow Jesus Christ, and now they were unemployed.

Who Were These Women?

In their state of mourning and shock, the disciples were only too glad to leave funeral preparations to the women. No one had any expectation that Jesus would **not** be dead forever. So when Mary the Mother of Jesus (Biblically defined as *the mother of James,"* one of Jesus' half-brothers), Mary Magdalene, Joanna (traditionally the wife of Simon Peter) and Salome crept down to the tomb early that Sunday morning, where they intended to perform the "last rites" for Jesus' Body.

His Mother was an obvious candidate for this task. Thirty-three years before, she had washed birth fluids from His newborn infant body, anointing Him with tiny dabs of myrrh (the gift from one of the Wise Men), and – since she was unavoidably far from her home in Nazareth when the Child was born, and therefore ill-equipped – she swaddled Him with long strips of borrowed cloth ... which were usually reserved for wrapping the dead. She had tended to His toddler body when He toppled over while learning to walk ... she had bandaged his pre-teen knees when He fell in a tumble of game-playing with His friends ... and she had hugged her precious Son when He finally became an adult. Now – here she was again – this time ready to wash, anoint, and wrap the Body of her Son for final burial.

Mary Magdalene was also a reasonable participant in the burial detail. Already she had unintentionally enacted the washing and anointing rites, when she had burst into the dinner at Simon the Leper's house (see Luke 7:36-50), and wept over Jesus' feet, drying them with her own hair. Then she broke open an alabaster box containing precious ointment and poured the contents onto Jesus' feet. She too had a tender heart toward Jesus and was honored to perform her last duty.

Many years ago, I wrote and produced a one-act Christian fictional drama entitled *"Another Chance,"* wherein I theorized about the identities of Joanna and Salome. In my play, Salome was a sister of Mary the Mother; therefore, as Jesus' aunt, she was fulfilling a noble family obligation. Joanna, however, was the long-suffering wife of Simon Peter, and – as a close friend of both the Marys and Salome, as well as the wife of Jesus' chief disciple – she has "business" to attend to before taking her broken-hearted husband back home to Galilee, where she hoped they would be able to resume "a normal life."

First Impressions Are Important

The women knew about the large stone blocking the tomb, and as they journeyed to the grave, they wondered what their options were.

Imagine their amazement when they arrived at the grave, only to find the stone displaced, all the guards sleeping unnaturally, the tomb itself empty ... except for a discarded winding-sheet. And an incandescently-clad young man – who was not Jesus Christ – casually sitting around, waiting for them!

As is often the case when the supernatural touches the lives of ordinary people, the angel's first words were: *"Don't be afraid!"* Glad will be the day when I can honestly say that fear is not my first reaction to the unexpected.

ය

[One more **fictional** short story to describe events around the Resurrection.]

Angel on Assignment

Charlie was busting his buttons with pride. He sat on the stone seat, arranging his robes neatly and precisely around him, sitting up posture per-fect. Then he jumped up and ran around the tiny, dark room, noting that the dirt floor was hard-packed – *"Not even any dust-bunnies to clean up!"* – and the walls were as smooth as hand-carved stone could be. *"Okay, nothing to do here."* He scrubbed his hands with his sleeve, removing the last of the grit from handling that large stone slab which was the door.

Charlie sat down again, and this time he crossed his knees, although he pulled his long robe down to cover his bare toes. Then he uncrossed his knees and again sat up straight and tall, so proud of this big responsibility. Then he jumped up and ran to the entrance of the room, cautiously peeking his head outside, spotting the huge stone door that had been pushed aside and now lay flat on the ground. *"Nope, still night-time, although I think it's getting close to dawn,"* he thought as he withdrew back inside.

His eyes were drawn to the faintly-shimmering cloth arranged long-ways on the bench which was part of the wall. He didn't dare touch it ... or maybe he could just tweak it a little bit? *"No! You know what Gabriel said to you, Charlie,"* he reminded himself. So he rubbed his hands together again, then clasped them tightly. He sat down again. *"It sure is quiet in here."*

Charlie thought back to just a few moments before, when he had first landed in this room. At that time he had discovered a figure laying per-fectly still on the bench, shrouded around with a long cloth: the corpse of an adult male human. A large handkerchief had been laid gently over the face. The whole room was totally dark, but Charlie didn't need earthly illumination to help him see since he was on assignment.

He had barely arrived when the ground began to tremble and shake ... and suddenly the room was flooded with brilliant light – so intense that even he had to squint against it – and then he watched as the long cloth on the bench subsided with a sigh, like a deflating balloon. The body was simply gone!

Instead, a strong and handsome Man stood there, stretching His arms high and wide, an incredibly joyous smile on His face. He was dressed in pure-white robes, which billowed and shimmered around His body as He turned in a little jig. Instantly, a tall angel appeared beside Him, and they grinned at each other. The Man shook hands with the Archangel, who immediately disappeared again.

Then the Man had turned and reached out to Charlie, ruffling his hair. "Hi, buddy!" the Son of God, the Prince of Heaven, the Commander-in-Chief said to him. "Thanks for meeting Me." From His pocket He pulled out the handkerchief which had previously covered His face, and He gave it to Charlie, with a wink of His brilliant eye. "And thanks for this, My friend. You truly helped Me back there in the Garden."

"He said that to ***me!"*** Charlie trembled even as he remembered the feeling of those strong

fingers touching his head. He recalled the condition of that hand: with a large, peculiar hole going right through. No blood, no bruising, no evident damage – just holes in each hand, and in each foot, indicating a mysterious transaction that had been completed.

Jesus had smiled once more at Charlie. "Gotta go, little buddy! See you soon!" And with that, He had vanished.

That had been Charlie's cue. He carefully folded his often-used handkerchief and laid it on top of the now-empty shroud, then he set about his main job: to remove the enormous stone that blocked the entrance of the room – or the grave, if it needed technical definition. The purpose was to permit entry for the humans who would shortly be arriving to pay their respects to the once-dead Man. Charlie chuckled, *"The Son of God did not need **any** help in getting **out**!"* Then he was to sit here and wait for people to show up. And to give them a message.

"Don't frighten them, Charlie," Gabriel had instructed him up in Heaven, before his Earth-side assignment began. "Humans are so easily freaked, so do your best to be calm and friendly. Then tell them: *'Do not be amazed. If you are looking for Jesus of Nazareth Who has been*

crucified, He is not here. He has risen from the
dead.' Give them time to work through that. If
they have questions, tell them, 'Remember that
He told you that the Son of Man would be delivered into the hands of sinful men, and would be
killed. And He told you that on the third day, He
would rise again. This is the third day – He has
risen!'"

The Archangel had paused, then added: "You
can also say, 'Jesus Christ will meet you in Galilee,
just as He already said.' Hopefully they will understand it all. Got it?" Charlie had nodded. "Repeat it all back to me, from the beginning!"
Gabriel had insisted. Charlie was so pleased with
himself because he was able to repeat every
detail of his assignment, he understood that the
timing which was so crucial, and the instructions
he was supposed to relay to the humans.

So now he was here, and half of his assignment was complete. All that was left to do was to
wait for the disciples to show up. One more time,
Charlie patted his handkerchief laying unneeded
on the deflated shroud, and then sat down again,
feeling very, very good.

He didn't notice that Gabriel had reappeared,
semi-transparently, standing behind him, holding

a check-list clipboard and a golden pen ... and an approving smile on his face.

છ

About the Lies

The high priests, scribes, Pharisees, and Sadducees were listening as closely to Jesus' teachings as the common people did. They heard Him claiming to be the Messiah,the Son of God. They heard Him warn about the three days to destroy the temple and then rebuild it. They knew He was proving the ancient prophecies one-by-one ... but still they feared Him.

Before the crucifixion, they knew the possibility existed that Jesus would return to life, and do it within three days. Before He was officially declared dead, they were back at Pilate's courtyard, currying favor with the Roman governor and "covering their butts," to put it plainly.

Pilate, again the consummate politician, knew he needed confirmation of the death of Jesus before he acted. There were three aspects of Jesus' tomb that were out-of-the-ordinary:

- the stone covering the tomb
- the seal over the tomb
- the guards on duty at the tomb.

Most Jewish tombs were closed with heavy wooden doors, hung on hinges. Only the wealthy could afford the stone "door," which was so heavy it would require several servants or workmen to budge this bulky slab. Once positioned, it was never supposed to be removed. Joseph of Arimathea was a wealthy man; his tomb was of polished stone, elaborately carved. The grave in which Jesus' Body was placed was not haphazard; it was designed to protect and to be permanent. This worked to the High Priest's advantage.

Knowing that Jesus' body was laid in a wealthy man's tomb, Pilate refused to dispatch any more Roman soldiers to handle this sticky situation, requiring the San Hedrin to assign their own troops to guard the tomb. They had brought this "Jesus problem" to him in first place – now they could deal with the ending themselves. The only part Pilate would participate in was ordering the tomb be sealed – not a typical treatment for Jewish graves.

The "seal" comes from the Greek word *sphragidzo,* meaning "a legal seal," such as was placed on documents, letters or possessions. The pur-pose was to authenticate that the "sealed item" had been properly inspected before sealing and that all the contents were in order. As long as the seal was unbroken, this guaranteed the contents inside were safe and undisturbed.

Most likely, the actual seal was a cord stretched tightly across the stone at the entrance of the tomb, held against the walls by fast-drying clay platelets positioned on either side, then imprinted before drying by Pilate's legal authorities using his official seal. Imprinting the official seal of the governor of Rome was the end of Roman involvement in Jesus' burial.

The guard detail, being Jewish soldiers, reported directly to the San Hedrin. They took their orders from the high priests, before and after Jesus' resurrection. The varying Gospels report their actions differently; some said the guards were sleeping, perhaps knocked unconscious, and others say they simply ran away when the stone rolled open by itself. Either way, they quickly hied back to their bosses, to report what they had witnessed.

It took the San Hedrin no time at all to decide their next move: cover-up, false reports and more dishonesty. They used the same strategy they had used to persuade Judas Iscariot to betray Jesus: they paid off the guards. They sent the hapless guards off on an endless sabbatical, with firm instructions to deceive: *"His disciples came by night and stole His body away, while we were asleep."* (What self-respecting soldier would actually admit to sleeping on the job?) The San Hedrin was terrified of what Pilate would do to **them** for "failing to protect the dead body" – and they were willing to lie to the whole world, but especially to Pilate.

Evidently the guards were better at spreading a lie than they were at guarding the tomb of a dead man (although how and why the tomb was opened required supernatural intervention), because *"this story was widely spread among the Jews, and is to this day."* **To this day,** in the 21st century, there are still people who do not believe Jesus Christ rose from the dead. I'd say the San Hedrin got their money's worth out of the bribes they paid to the guards, a wicked transaction that reverberates through the millennia.

Mary and the "Gardener"

Again, each Gospel reports the way the women found the empty tomb differently. The report about Mary Magdalene was especially poignant and totally believable: a sorrowing woman so grief-stricken she couldn't see what is actually in front of her (although I suppose if I was met by two angels, I might be flustered too). She was over-whelmed by her tears, and had wanted to know one thing only: *"Where was the Body of Jesus?"*

There is a lovely old hymn derived from this story:

I come to the Garden alone
While the dew is still on the roses
And the Voice I hear, calling on my ear
The Son of God discloses

And He walks with me, and He talks with me
And He tells me I am His own
And the joy we share as we tarry there
None other has ever known
He speaks, and the sound of His voice

Is so sweet, the birds hush their singing
And the melody that He gave to me
Within my heart is ringing

I'd stay in the Garden with Him
Though the night around me be falling
But He bids me go, through the Voice of woe
His Voice to me is calling.

– Charles Austin Miles

The Voice that spoke to Mary in the garden by the tomb still speaks to those who love Him, who search for Him today.

Jesus Had a Sense of Humor (Emmaus)

This may be a little irreverent, but I have often had the mental image of this passage from Luke 24 being played out by the old-time comedians Abbott and Costello (famous for the *"Who's On First?"* comedy sketch), while Jesus plays the "straight man." The two travelers, Cleopas and another unnamed man, were so deep into their conversation about Jesus that they failed to recognize Him when He joined them in their travels ... although I suspect He may have been wearing a hood over his head that obscured His face, so He could take the pulse of the general population about His crucifixion and – more importantly – His resurrection:

They were talking with each other about everything that had happened. As they

*talked and discussed these things with each other, Jesus Himself came up walked walked along with them; but **they were kept from recognizing Him.***
Luke 24:14-16; emphasis added

How often have we wished we could be with Jesus Christ in person! Wouldn't it be wonderful to look at Him face-to-face, asking Him our personal questions and hearing His wise responses, sitting near Him while He teaches? What would be the first thing **you** said to Jesus, if you were walking with Him along the road to Emmaus? Those people who were alive in the First Century were so privileged to hear His actual voice and recognize His actual features!

Throughout history, artists have attempted to capture the appearance of Jesus, and so we have a variety of styles; sometimes He looks very Caucasian, other times very Middle Eastern, sometimes we've seen Him depicted in cartoons. However, there is one authentic representation of the human face of Jesus in the amazing imprint on the world-famous Shroud of Turin:

The Shroud of Turin is a linen cloth bearing the image of a man who appears to have suffered physical trauma in a manner consistent with crucifixion. It is kept in the Royal Chapel of the Cathedral of Saint John the Baptist in Turin, northern Italy. The image on the shroud is commonly associated with Jesus Christ, His crucifixion and burial. It is much clearer in black-and-white negative than in its natural sepia color.

My brother-in-law, Dr. Phillip H. Wiebe, is a respected Professor of Philosophy at *Trinity Western University* in Langley, British Columbia, Canada; he is also an expert on many aspects of the Shroud of Turin, and frequently lectures on its validity and importance to Christianity. That we can see the imprint of the face of our Lord and Savior Jesus Christ still on the Shroud today is so profoundly wonderful! Our next experience of seeing Him alive and well, face-to-face, will be that glorious day when we all pass from life, through death, into Life Eternal!

We know we **can** walk hand-in-hand with Jesus Christ every day of our lives, and we **can** speak directly to Him from the depths of our hearts. This conversation is called prayer.

This is the confidence we have in approaching God: that if we ask anything according to His will, He hears us. And if we know that He hears us – whatever we ask – we know that we have what we asked of Him.
1 John 5:14-15

Every day can be like walking with Jesus Christ along the roads of life. And He may just "pull a

Behold the Lamb ~ 224

prank" on us too, to show that He too has a sense of humor!

"Blessed Are Those Who Have Not Seen ..."

Oh, that Thomas Didymus! He seems so much like too many people today: stubbornly refusing to believe – to accept the news of Christ's resurrection by faith – digging in his heels until he was given irrefutable proof!

Child-like faith is a highly-valued attribute. The innocence, non-judgmental trust that a young girl knows in her heart, relying on her mother to do what she says she will do – this is how simple our faith in God needs to be:

> *People were bringing little children to Jesus for Him to place His hands on them, but the disciples rebuked them. When Jesus saw this, He was indignant. He said to them, "Let the little children come to Me, and do not hinder them for the Kingdom of God belongs to such as these. Truly I tell you: anyone who will not receive the Kingdom of God like a little child will never enter it." And He took the children in His arms, placed His hands on them and blessed them.*
>
> **Mark 10:13-16**

It's easy to imagine Thomas Didymus might have been one of those grumpy disciples who were rebuking the children, who just didn't comprehend what Jesus was trying to tell him: at all times, in every situation, no matter how impossible life seems to be, God is with us, He cares for us, He knows every detail of our lives, He can see into the deepest part of our hearts, and He **will** see His plan for our lives brought to fulfillment:

Being confident of this, that He Who began a good work in you will carry it on to completion until the day of Christ Jesus.
Philippians 1:6

The famed 19th century writer, Sir James M. Barrie, admitted that for his classic book *"Peter Pan,"* he got the idea for the three human children – Wendy Darling, John Darling and baby brother Michael Darling – by connecting the passages from Mark 10 and John 20. Sir James believed in child-like faith, and his most apt illustration of this was when Tinker Bell, the tiny fairy who is a friend of Peter Pan, sprinkled fairy dust onto the human children so they were able to fly. However John Darling, the middle child, really struggled with this idea, and repeatedly failed to launch into the air. He is encouraged to keep on trying when *Peter Pan* says, *"All it takes is faith, hope and trust ... and a little bit of fairy dust!"*

For Thomas Didymus, it required Jesus Christ Himself saying to him, *"Stop doubting and believe. ... Because you have seen Me, you have believed. Blessed are those who have not seen and yet have believed"* (John 20:27b, 29). We don't need "fairy dust" to bolster our faith in Christ; we need to find the child-like part inside our hearts and let that take charge. **Jesus takes us in His arms and blesses *us*.**

Jesus and Simon Peter

This is one of the most heart-wrenching yet heart-warming parts of the Bible: the reconciliation of friends.

Jesus knew Peter so well – knew his volatile personality, knew his strengths and his failings, knew his *joie de vivre* and his obstinacy, but mostly knew more deeply into his heart than Peter knew himself – and as much as their friendship had been strong and sweet, Jesus knew that Peter had frailties. Those weaknesses would cause him – the boastful, self-confident man who insisted: "Jesus, I shall **never** betray You" – to betray Him. Not once, but three times in a very short span.

When Jesus met Peter and the other disciples on the beach at the Sea of Tiberias, there were some similarities to previous land-and-sea experiences they had shared: Jesus helped them improve their fishing (again) ... Peter impetuously jumped out of the boat because he was so eager to see Jesus ... God's Son proved Himself a Master Chef as He hand-prepared breakfast for His friends – serving them fish and bread, so reminiscent of that wonderful "feeding 5,000" experience.

It was in a somewhat private moment when Jesus drew alongside His dear friend and gave him the opportunity to repent sincerely and forever for the agony of betrayal. To hammer the point home, Jesus asked him the same question three times: *"Do you love Me?"* – because, of course, Peter had denied his Friend three times just a few days before. We can see Peter's face flushing at the question, his head hanging, finding it difficult to meet his Master's eyes. By the third query, however, it was apparent that Jesus was doing more than patching up a damaged personal relationship: He has already forgiven him, and to demonstrate His trust in Peter, Jesus Christ was commissioning him to become the flag-bearer of His Gospel.

Years later, Peter would allude to this time in his life:

> *And the God of all grace, Who called you to His eternal glory in Christ, after you have suffered a little while* **will Himself restore you** *and make you strong, firm and steadfast.*
> **1 Peter 5:10; emphasis added**

The broad shoulders of the fisherman from Galilee **would** be able to fulfill the heavy responsibility Jesus placed on him. How do we know? Luke the Physician wrote glowingly about the Fisherman in the Book of Acts: of his boldness, his perseverance and discernment, his natural leadership abilities, his strong anointing:

When they saw the courage of Peter and John, and realized they were unschooled, ordinary men, they were astonished, and they took note that these men had been with Jesus.

Acts 4:13

"He's just a fisherman, not educated"? Didn't matter – Peter had been with Jesus. *"Blows hot and cold, unstable personality"?* Didn't matter – **Peter had been with Jesus!**

*At the hands of the apostles, many signs and wonders were taking place among the people; and they were all with one accord in Solomon's Portico. ... And all the more believers in the Lord, multitudes of men and women, were constantly added to their number, to such an extent that they even carried the sick out into the streets and laid them on cots and pallets so that **when Peter came by, at least his shadow might fall on any one of them** ... and they were all being healed.*

Acts 5:12-16; emphasis added

Another reason Jesus asked this question of Peter was trifold: first, to secure their personal relationship; second, to secure his ministry to the Jews; third, to secure his ministry to the Gentiles.

His Last Instructions

Jesus came to Earth with one assignment: to die in payment for the sins for all Mankind. His assignment completed, now He mobilized the disciples who had traveled with Him for three years, who had heard Him teach and seen Him perform miracles, He had taken time to unravel for them the "mysteries" held within the parables He preached ... and had seen Him arrested unjustly, beaten and maligned cruelly, tried in court three times and sentenced to death. Some had trailed along the streets of Jerusalem as He dragged His cross to Golgotha, and had watched Him die. And then witnessed His return to life! They had fellow-shipped closely with Him, basking in His presence, being His confidantes and companions.

Their relationship and responsibilities did not stop there. It did not end when Jesus ascended into Heaven, leaving them behind on Earth. He gave them an assignment, every one of them ... and everyone who, in the two millennium since He walked on Earth, believe in Him. We, like the disciples, now carry a solemn responsibility: to tell the whole world about Him!

The Upper Room

When the disciples saw Jesus ascending into Heaven, rising upward on billowing white clouds, this time the parting was not filled with the horror of death (the crucifixion) or the realization of separation, but they had a sense of acceptance that this is how God had meant it to be all along. It was more like the fond farewell of a passenger boarding a cruise ship, where we – the people left standing on the dock – know that the passenger was embarking on a wonderful experience, and we wish them an enjoyable journey although we ourselves are going to stay here and go about our regular lives.

Of course, Jesus had already told them He wasn't just going to be sitting around idly in Heaven:

"Do not let your hearts be troubled. You believe in God, believe also in Me. My Father's House has many rooms; if that were not so, would I have told you that I am going there to prepare a place for you? And if I go and prepare a place for you, I will come back and take you to be with Me that you also may be where I am. You know the way to the place where I am going."

John 14:1-4

This is the heart and purpose of the Gospel message: *"You know the way to the place where I am going"* (verse 4) – Jesus **IS** the Way! This was the mandate of the disciples in 33 AD, and it is the mandate of **all** believers (not just the laity) today: to tell the whole world that the **only** way we will ever connect again with God Almighty is through the cross of Jesus Christ, where the Lamb of God came to take away the sins of the world. Our job is to populate Heaven!

In the Upper Room – a place where once they had dined with Jesus ... where He had washed their feet ... later, where they had hidden and mourned His death ... and later still, where He "walked through walls" to appear to them again – now the disciples obeyed His command:

> *"I am going to send you what My Father has promised; but stay in the city until you have been clothed with power from on high."*
>
> **Luke 24:49**

> *"You will receive power when the Holy Spirit comes on you; and you will be My witnesses in Jerusalem, and in all Judea and Samaria, and to the ends of the Earth."*
>
> **Acts 1:8**

The Holy Spirit, of course, is the presence of Jesus Christ living within them – and within us. He is as alive and well and active today as He was in 33 AD! What He did through the disciples then was phenomenal, goals that we should be striving to meet and exceed:

> *When the day of Pentecost came, they were all together in one place. Suddenly a sound like the blowing of a violent wind came from Heaven and filled the whole house where they were sitting. They saw*

what seemed to be tongues of fire that separated and came to rest on each of them. All of them were filled with the Holy Spirit, and began to speak in other tongues as the Spirit enabled them.

Now there were staying in Jerusalem God-fearing Jews from every nation under Heaven. When they heard this sound, a crowd came together in bewilderment, because each one heard their own language being spoken. Utterly amazed, they asked, "Aren't all these who are speaking Galileans? Then how it is that each of us hears them in our native language? Parthians, Medes and Elamites, residents of Mesopotamia, Judea and Cappodocia, Pontus and Asia, Phrygia and Pamphylia, Egypt and the part of Libya near Cyrene, visitors from Rome (both Jews and converts to Judaism), Cretans and Arabs -- we hear them declaring the wonders of God in our own tongues!" Amazed and perplexed, they asked one another, "What does this mean?" Some, however, made fun of them and said, "They have had too much wine."

Then Peter stood up with the Eleven, raised his voice and addressed the crowd: "Fellow Jews and all of you who live in Jerusalem, let me explain this to you; listen carefully to what I say. These people are not drunk, as you suppose. It's only nine in the morning!

No, this is what was spoken by the prophet Joel:

*"'In the last days, God says, I will pour out My Spirit on all people. Your sons and daughters will prophesy, your young men will see visions, your old men will dream dreams. Even on My servants, both men and women, I will pour out My Spirit in those days, and they will prophesy. I will show wonders in the Heavens above and signs on the Earth below, blood and fire and billows of smoke. The sun will be turned to darkness and the moon to blood, before the coming of the great and glorious day of the Lord. **And everyone who calls on the Name of the Lord will be saved.'***

*"Fellow Israelites, listen to this: Jesus of Nazareth was a Man accredited by God to you by miracles, wonders and signs, which God did among you through Him, as you yourselves know. This Man was handed over to you **by God's deliberate plan and foreknowledge;** and you, with the help of wicked men, put Him to death by nailing Him to the cross. But God raised Him from the dead, freeing Him from the agony of death, because it was impossible for death to keep its hold on Him. ... Therefore, let all Israel be assured of this: God has made this Jesus, Whom you crucified, both Lord and Messiah."*

When the people heard this, they were cut to the heart, and said to Peter and the other apostles, "Brothers, what shall we do?"

Peter replied, "Repent and be baptized, every one of you, in the Name of Jesus Christ, for the forgiveness of your sins. And you will receive the gift of the Holy Spirit. The promise is for you and your children, and for all who are far off – for all whom the Lord our God will call." With many other words he warned them, and he pleaded with them, "Save yourselves from this corrupt generation." Those who accepted his message were baptized, and **about three thousand were added to their number THAT DAY.**

They devoted themselves to the apostles' teaching and to fellowship, to the breaking of bread and to prayer. Everyone was filled with awe at the many wonders and signs performed by the apostles. All the believers were together and had everything in common. They sold property and possessions to give to anyone who had need. Every day they continued to meet together in the Temple courts. They broke bread in their homes and ate together with glad and sincere hearts, praising God and enjoying the favor of all the people. And the Lord added to their number daily those who

were being saved.
Acts 2:1-25, 36-47; emphasis added

My friend **Andraé Crouch** wrote about this event in his vivacious song *"I've Got It!"*:

When the Day of Pentecost had come
They were in the Upper Room with one accord
They gathered together, one-hundred-and-twenty
To receive the power God promised to send
The Holy Ghost fell upon each one
As the Spirit made them rich, they spoke in tongues

There in the city, men from everywhere
They couldn't understand what was happening up there
Then Peter stood in the midst of the crowd
He spoke with a voice that was clear and loud
He said, "This is that spoken by the Prophet Joel
"That in the last days, My Spirit I'll outpour
"Not only to me, but also to you
"Every child of God that wants to go through!"

I've got it, I've got it
I've got it, I've got it
Something about the power of the Holy Ghost
I can't explain it
But I've got it, I've got it!

Jesus is the Lamb of God Whose sole purpose on Earth was to pay our debt of sin. He came from Heaven and lived among humans for 33 years, and specifically ministered to them for three years – teaching, healing, performing miracles – and enjoying the fellowship of His twelve chosen disciples and all who believed and followed Him. Never once did He deviate from the goal – to die for them – because His plans did not stop at the door of death. His plans continue to unfold in our lives as we answer the assignment:

> *Go into all the world and preach the Good News of Jesus Christ, the Messiah, the Son of God, the Lamb of God Who takes away all our sins.*

Amen!

Epilogue

THE SUFFERING OF JESUS CHRIST
Reprinted from *e-Jeanne: 2004 (Part One)* ~
Posted 18 February 2004

[**INTRODUCTION:** In 2004, when I was publish-
ing my weekly "newsletter" (before blogs were
invented) *e-Jeanne*, all the world was antici-pating
Mel Gibson's landmark movie *"The Passion of the
Christ."* (This was long before Mel "fell from
grace"; we can only hope he has been reconciled
with Christ since then.) This article is an e-
Editorial from that time.]

    I had intended to publish the text of the *ABC
Primetime* Interview which aired on Monday night,
between Diane Sawyer and Mel Gibson regarding
The Passion of the Christ, but I discovered that
ABC-News's once-free transcription service now
costs $20 a pop … so I guess not. But what I will
do is give some of my own impressions of that

national TV interview which had been loudly and much advertised.

The main problem is that the Secular Press just don't get it: Jesus Christ was crucified by **all of us.** We are all to blame for sin ... it's been built-in since that fateful day in the Garden of Eden. Jesus was "condemned to death" **by God** – He is the One Who sent His own Son to die in our place:

> *For God so loved the world that He* **gave** *His only begotten Son, that whoever believes in Him should not perish but have everlasting life. For God did not send His Son into the world to condemn the world, but that the world* **through Him** *might be saved.*
>
> **John 3:16-17; NKJV**

Isn't that the most fundamental lesson Christians are taught from infancy? The secular press have blown up a smoke screen – all the emphasis on whether Mel Gibson and his movie are anti-Semitic or not – rather than face the truth: Jesus was crucified by **every single one of us,** because we are sinners lost from God unless we understand and accept the enormous sacrifice He made for us. And Jesus just didn't pop into the world and live among humans for 33 years, then blipped Himself into oblivion and returned to His Home ... He **suffered** greatly – emotionally, spiritually, intellectually, and physically – in order to purchase our salvation.

At the top of Diane's interview, she mentioned that Mel uses the word "passion" in its original, correct Greek meaning: *pathos,* meaning "suffering." That is what this movie is actually about. It is finally stripping away all the social niceties of avoiding the physical cruelty and gore that surrounded Jesus' beatings, humiliations, abuses, tortures, and agonizing death. We've been such a sheltered society all these thousands of years that we've draped a rag of cloth over Jesus' genitals rather than show Him naked, which is actually the way He was crucified. No strategic-ally-placed and almost-spotlessly clean garment obscuring nudity in order to get a PG-13 rating – this R-rated (for violence) movie instead has gouts of blood dripping so profusely, such badly bruised flesh, and the shocked, pain-crazed expression on His face that we cringe to even look at Him, and perhaps don't even notice that He is naked.

> *He has no form or comeliness; and when we see Him, there is no beauty that we should desire Him. He is despised and rejected by men, a Man of sorrows and acquainted with grief. And we hid, as it were, our faces from Him; He was despised, and we did not esteem Him.*
> **Isaiah 53:2-3; NKJV**

> *There was nothing attractive about Him, nothing to cause us to take a second look. He was looked down on and passed over, a Man Who suffered, Who knew pain firsthand. One look at Him and people*

turned away.   We looked down on Him, thought He was scum.
                                                      Isaiah 53:2-3; the Message

   This movie makes us begin to realize that Jesus had ample opportunities to "escape" His fate, but chose not to. He faced it directly, even deliberately moving toward it. Talk about purpose-driven life!

- From the moment in Heaven when He volunteered to become the Ultimate Sacrifice for Mankind and His Father agreed to permit it [*"Worthy is the Lamb Who was slain, to receive power and riches and wisdom, and strength and honor and glory and blessing!"* (Revelation 5:12)].

- ... throughout His childhood [*"I must be about My Father's business"* (Luke 2:49)] and ministry [*"You know that after two days is the Passover, and the Son of Man will be delivered up to be crucified"* (Matthew 26:2) ... *"For this is My Blood of the New Covenant, which is shed for many for the remission of sins"* (Matthew 26:28)].

- ... and even when there was that one little almost-glitch (which proved that He was completely human, He was God-in-**flesh**) in the Garden of Gethsemane [*"O My Father, if this cup cannot pass away from Me unless I drink it, Your will be done"* (Matthew 26:42)].

- ... and when He plainly told the disciples not to interfere with His accusers and arresters [*"Or do you think that I cannot now pray to My Father, and He will provide Me with more than twelve legions of angels? How then could the Scriptures be fulfilled, that it must happen thus?"* (Matthew 26:53-54)].

The fact is: **Jesus was born to die,** and **all of Mankind** are the ones who killed Him.

Did He expect His punishment and death to be so cruel and have so much suffering involved? Absolutely He knew: *"My soul is exceedingly sorrowful, even to death. Stay here and watch with Me. ... O My Father, if it is possible, let this cup pass from Me; nevertheless, not as I will, but as You will"* (Matthew 26:38-39). And that is what Mel Gibson wanted to portray in this movie. The *"Passion of the Christ"* means *"the **suffering** which Jesus Christ willingly undertook to provide salvation for all Mankind,"* for all who will experience this dramatic and violent portrayal of those events and who will not count it as worthless or irrelevant to each of us individually. Mel even said that to Diane: "We are all of us to blame for Christ's death."

I don't know if Mel then proceeded to lay out the "Four Spiritual Laws" or the "Roman Road" to Diane – that might have ended up on the cutting-room floor – but personally, I intend to be prepared to look carefully and deliberately into the faces of my fellow movie-goers, to see if there's someone who has been shocked into realizing that Jesus died for him or her, and am willing to offer a shoulder to weep on or a hand to hold … and a gentle-but-firm voice to say, "I can help you find this Jesus as your Savior." I believe that hearts will be softened because of this movie, and I believe the church has a responsibility to use this opportunity to win souls.

Also I know that, eventually, the Secular Media **will** get it … either now, in this life, or when they stand before the Judgment Seat of God and are asked, "So what did **you** do with My Son, Jesus the Christ?"

This Season of the Lamb is going to be one of the greatest experiences any of us have ever known. We will remember the betrayal, trumped-up trials, beatings, tortures, humiliations, abuses, cruelties, and execution of "Good Friday" with a realism we've never known before … and we will rejoice in the triumphant Resurrection, in the finished work that Jesus Christ did:

> *"You are worthy to take the scroll and open its seals, for You were slain, and have redeemed us to God by Your Blood out of every tribe and tongue and people and nation. And have made us kings and priests to our God, and we shall reign on the Earth. … Worthy is the Lamb Who was slain to receive power and riches and wisdom, and strength and honor and glory and blessing! … Blessing and honor and*

glory and power be to Him Who sits on the Throne, and to the Lamb forever and ever!"
Revelation 5:9-13

The success of this movie is going to be counted in redeemed souls. Amen! – **Jeanne, e-Editor**

c103

[In that same 18 February 2004 edition of *e-Jeanne,* I posted the following true story.]

THE EMPTY EASTER EGG
Author Unknown

Jeremy Forrester was born with a twisted body and a slow mind. At the age of 12, he was still in Second Grade, seemingly unable to learn. His teacher, Doris Miller, often became exasperated with him. He would squirm in his seat, drool, and make grunting noises. At other times, he spoke clearly and distinctly, as if a spot of light had penetrated the darkness of his brain. Most of the time, however, Jeremy just irritated his teacher.

One day she called his parents and asked them to come in for a consultation. As the Forresters entered the empty classroom, Doris said to them, "Jeremy really belongs in a special school. It isn't fair to him to be with younger children who don't have learning problems. Why, there is a five year gap between his age and that of the other students."

Mrs. Forrester cried softly into a tissue, while her husband spoke. "Miss Miller," he said, "there is no school of that kind nearby. It would be a terrible shock for Jeremy if we had to take him out of this school. We know he really likes it here."

Doris sat for a long time after they had left, staring at the snow outside the window. Its cold-ness seemed to seep into her soul. She wanted to sympathize with the Forresters. After all, their only child had a terminal illness. But it wasn't fair to keep him in her class. She had eighteen other youngsters to teach, and Jeremy was a distrac-tion. Furthermore, he would never learn to read and write. Why waste any more time trying?

As she pondered the situation, guilt washed over her. "Here I am," she thought. "Lord, please help me to be more patient with Jeremy." From that day on, she tried hard to ignore Jeremy's noises and his blank stares.

Then one day, he limped to her desk, dragging his bad leg behind him. "I love you, Miss Miller," he exclaimed, loud enough for the whole class to hear. The other students snickered, and Doris' face turned red.

She stammered, "Why, that's very nice, Jeremy. Now, please take your seat."

Spring came, and the children talked excitedly about the coming of Easter. Doris told them the story of Jesus, and then to emphasize the idea of new life springing forth, she gave each of the children a large plastic egg. "Now," she said to them, "I want you to take this home and bring it back tomorrow with something inside that shows new life. Do you understand?"

"Yes, Miss Miller," the children responded enthusiastically – all except for Jeremy. He listened intently; his eyes never left her face. He did not even make his usual noises. Had he understood what she had said about Jesus' death and resurrection? Did he understand the assignment? Perhaps she should call his parents and explain the project to them.

That evening, Doris' kitchen sink stopped up. She called the landlord, and waited an hour for him to come by and unclog it. After that, she still had to shop for groceries, iron a blouse, and prepare a vocabulary test for the next day. She completely forgot about phoning Jeremy's parents.

The next morning, nineteen children came to school, laughing and talking as they placed their eggs in the large wicker basket on Miss Miller's desk. After they completed their Math lesson, it was time to open the eggs. In the first egg, Doris found a flower. "Oh, yes, a flower is certainly a sign of new life," she exclaimed to the class. "When plants peek through the ground, we know that Spring is here."

A small girl in the first row waved her arm. "That's my egg, Miss Miller," she called out.

The next egg contained a plastic butterfly, which looked very real. Doris held it up. "We all know that a caterpillar changes and grows into a beautiful butterfly. Yes, that's new life too."

Little Judy smiled proudly and said, "Miss Miller, that one is mine."

Next, Doris found a rock with moss on it. She explained that moss too showed life. Billy spoke up from the back of the classroom, "My Daddy helped me," he beamed.

Then Doris opened the fourth egg. She gasped. The egg was empty. "Surely it must be Jeremy's," she thought, "and of course, he did not understand my instructions. If only I had not forgotten to phone his parents!" Because she did not want to embarrass him, she quietly set the egg aside and reached for another.

Suddenly, Jeremy spoke up, quite clearly, "Miss Miller, aren't you going to talk about my egg?"

Flustered, Doris replied, "But, Jeremy, your egg is empty."

He looked into her eyes and said softly, "Yes, but Jesus' tomb was empty too."

Time stopped. When she could speak again, Doris asked him, "Do you know why the tomb was empty?"

"Oh, yes," Jeremy said, "Jesus was killed and put in there. Then His Father raised Him up."

The recess bell rang. While the children excitedly ran out to the schoolyard, Doris cried. The cold inside her melted completely away.

Three months later, Jeremy died. Those who paid there respects at the mortuary were surprised to see nineteen eggs on top of his casket, all of them empty.

Are You Ready?

Do you know Jesus Christ? What a privilege it would have been to be chosen as one of His twelve disciples ... or to have been among the 5,000 who heard Him speak on a mountainside ... or to have seen Him healing the sick or raising the dead ... or to have sat close to Him and asked Him questions about the Kingdom of God! But He did not only exist in the first century and we read about Him in the pages of a Book – He is alive and well today! And we **can** know Him through the agency of His Holy Spirit:

> *The Advocate, the Holy Spirit Whom the Father will send in My Name, will teach you all things and will remind you of everything I*

*have said of you. Peace I leave with you;
My peace I give to you. I do not give to you
as the world gives. Do not let your hearts
be troubled and do not be afraid.*

John 14:26-27

The people who lived in the First Century struggled to understand Who Jesus was, but we have
the benefit of two thousand-plus years to see the
whole picture: that indeed He was the holy, sinless Son of God Who came with one specific purpose – to pay **our** debt of sin once and forever –
and He fulfilled that transaction perfectly, flawless-
ly, on the cross at Golgotha. The Lamb of God
gave up His life as the final sacrifice ... God accepted His sacrifice and opened the way into
Heaven ... and we can now accept that offer to be
joined with Almighty God for eternity.

"How do I do that, Jeanne?" I'm glad you
asked! First, answer these questions:

**(1) Do you believe Jesus Christ is the Son of
God?**

*For God so love the world that He gave His
one and only Son, that whoever believes in
Him shall not perish but have Eternal Life.
For God did not send His Son into the world
to condemn the world, but to save the world
through Him.*

John 3:16-17

(2) Do you believe He came to die for you, to pay your debt of sin?

If we confess our sins, He is faithful and just and will forgive us our sins and purify us from all unrighteousness.

1 John 1:9

(3) Do you believe all your sins are forgiven because of Christ's sacrifice?

Everyone who calls on the Name of the Lord will be saved.

Romans 10:13

(4) Do you believe God raised Jesus Christ from the dead?

If you confess with your mouth that Jesus is Lord and believe in your heart that God raised Him from the dead, you will be saved.

Romans 10:9

(5) Are you ready to give your heart to Jesus, to live for Him?

It's in Christ that we find out who we are and what we are living for. Long before we first heard of Christ and got our hopes up, He had His eye on us, had designs on us for glorious living, part of the overall purpose He is working out in everything and everyone.

Ephesians 1:11-12; the Message

If you answered "Yes" to those questions, then open your heart and pray this prayer:

*"Dear Jesus – Now I understand Who You are, why You came to Earth, what You did on my behalf. I know that You love me, and I want to learn to love You. I believe you are the Son of God. My life has been filled with sin, but there is no sin too big or too ugly or too strong that Your sacrifice on the cross does not wash away. I am sorry for my sins ... and I accept Your forgiveness. Wash me and make me presentable to Your Father – to **my** Heavenly Father – and come into my heart. I give Your Holy Spirit permission to live inside of me, helping, teaching, strengthening, filling me as I learn to become more like You. Thank You for dying for me; help me to live for You. Amen!"*

Welcome to our big, wonderful, real-life family, the active-duty Army of God! Now tell somebody what you have done! Tell me via e-mail – halseywrite@comcast.net – and find a Bible-believing church, find a Christian friend, but get planted in the family of God as quickly as possible (we have enemies, so you need to be surrounded by believers).

My prayer for you is that the Lamb of God will become the Best Friend you have ever had.

Musical Addendum

As I was completing the manuscript, I realized that in addition to *"Behold the Lamb,"* there are many other Season of the Lamb songs I love to sing. In an Editorial of *e-Jeanne* dated March 9, 2005, I included several of these songs, with little vignettes describing their personal importance. Here are a few of them – and I encourage you, the Reader, to sing these songs with your family.

ଔ

While I always revel in the giddiness of Christmas, I solemnly and gratefully honor and celebrate the reason why that tiny God-and-Man Baby was born: He was born to die for me. And for you. Christmas holds so many wonderful memories, but so does the Season of the Lamb, especially starting back at my childhood.

Most of us can wander back to childhood memories that will include something like a little country church with maybe a piano and sometimes an organ too, and a simple congregation singing:

The Old Rugged Cross

On a hill far away stood an old rugged cross
The emblem of suffering and shame
And I love that old cross
Where the dearest and best
For a world of lost sinners was slain

So I'll cherish the old rugged cross
Till my trophies at last I lay down
I will cling to the old rugged cross
And exchange it some day for a crown

Oh that old rugged cross
So despised by the world
Has a wondrous attraction for me
For the dear Lamb of God left His glory above
To bear it to dark Calvary

In that old rugged cross
Stained with blood so divine
A wondrous beauty I see
For 'twas on that old cross
Jesus suffered and died
To pardon and sanctify me

To the old rugged cross I will ever be true
Its shame and reproach gladly bear
Then He'll call me some day to my home far away
Where His glory forever I'll share.

– George Bennard

When I entered my teens, a bright new group, *The Second Chapter of Acts,* brought a fresh perspective to my Season of the Lamb celebrations:

The Easter Song

Hear the bells ringing, they're singing that you can be born again

Hear the bells ringing, they're singing Christ is
risen from the dead
The angel up on the tombstone said, "He has
risen, just as He said
"Quickly now, go tell His disciples that Jesus Christ
is no longer dead

"Joy to the world, He has risen, hallelujah
He's risen, hallelujah, He's risen, hallelujah!"

Hear the bells ringing, they're singing that you can
be healed right now
Hear the bells ringing, they're singing, Christ, He
will reveal it now
The angels, they all surround us, and they are
ministering Jesus' power
Quickly now, reach out and receive it, for this
could be your glorious hour.

– Annie Herring

I used to blast that song on the record-player (yes, I am seriously dating myself!) early Sunday morning to awaken my family to the joyous celebration awaiting us. Somehow **Kenneth** and I managed to de-emphasize bunnies and chicks and colorful eggs to our children **Jennifer** and **Alexander,** rather pointing them to a Risen Savior. In later years, we played and sang:

Jesus Is Alive

Hallelujah, Jesus is alive
Death has lost its victory

And the grave has been denied
Jesus lives forever, He's alive, He's alive.
He's the Alpha and Omega
The First and Last is He
The curse of sin is broken
And we have perfect liberty
The Lamb of God is risen
He's alive, He's alive
Hallelujah, Jesus is alive.

– Ron Kenoly

The funny thing about this "Memory Lane" is that I cannot remember one single time of walking through the local shopping mall and hearing any one of these songs playing sweetly in the background as ambient music (to encourage me to spend my money). In fact, the secular world has missed out on any genuine understanding of why we honor the death of a Man over 2,000 years ago, or why we know He is alive today. Maybe they "get" the birth of Jesus Christ, but they certainly don't understand His death and resurrection.

☙

There is a new Season of the Lamb song I have recently learned; unless you have a unique voice and talent like Annie Wolaver Dupre of *The Annie Moses Band,* it might be difficult to sing corporately, but it certainly ministers individually:

Tough As Nails

His heart was kind, strength was in His eyes
He wore no disguise, He had a mission
He spoke no words as they mocked and hit
But He set His face like flint
And it didn't matter
He knew what He was after

And His heart broke, and His breath choked
And the whip did rip with a meat-stroke
And His flesh tore, and His blood poured
And our sins dug in like a sharp thorn
But He did not fight when the hammer fell
His love was tough as nails, tough as nails
His love was tough as nails

He took the cross, stumbled up the hill
He would not quit until the work was finished
The day turned dark
And the hammer pounded pain
Then His final answer rang, "Father, forgive them"
And the Love of loves drove Him

And His heart broke, and His breath choked
And the whip did rip with a meat-stroke
And His flesh tore, and His blood poured
And our sins dug in like a sharp cord
But He did not fight when the hammer fell
His love was tough as nails, tough as nails
His love was tough as nails.

– Robin Wolaver and Benjamin Wolaver

For all the songwriters who may read this book, let me offer this encouragement: **write us some new Season of the Lamb songs!**

Resources

Acknowledgements and Dedication

In 1994, my pastor asked me to write a "Season of the Lamb" Devotional for our congregation, especially one which could be undertaken as families. With such a wide age-range in mind, I set out to analyze this beloved story, primarily focusing on the account from the Gospel of Mark, and to write it so all ages could receive something fresh, provocative, entertaining, enlightening, inspirational. This book was born out of that project, so I must first thank my pastor and friend **Dr. Kim O. Ryan** for his suggestions and contributions, his insight and input, and his frequent-yet-gentle urgings that I finish the original devotional on time.

My elder sister **Judy A. Gossett** read the initial draft, and presented thoughtful suggestions and strengthening encouragement which made me really want to complete the manuscript. We talked about the many Seasons of the Lamb we had experienced together, and she reminded me of several significant points in this story. Now that she is celebrating face-to-face with our Lord and Savior Jesus Christ (having gone Home to Heaven in 2003), I suspect she is still smiling at me with her twinkling green eyes, glad that this project has at last come to life.

My Other Sister **Reba Rambo-McGuire** sang with her lovely, silvery soprano voice the hauntingly beautiful lyrics of the song, *"Behold the Lamb,"* which her mother Dottie Rambo had written, and from which I took the title for this book. While writing, I programmed my laptop to play that song for hours; Reba's music kept the flavor of this book alive and on course. In 2013, Reba has taken over as chief proof-reader, brilliant suggestions-maker and faithful encourager ... and I am eternally indebted to my beloved Other Sister!

I thought this manuscript was lost forever until my dear friend **Lisa Nymeyer** uncovered it in a box of electrical wiring (who in the world put it in *there*?). It is without hesi-tation – and a great deal of happiness – that I dedicate this book to her:

Dear Lisa,

*As you continue in your walk with Jesus Christ, your Savior, your Lord, your Risen King, the Lamb of God, I pray that He is real to you and with you today and forever. It will be my honor to again share Holy Communion sitting on the edge of my bathtub, and one day to rejoice as you walk into the waters of baptism, to rise again as the 'new creation in Christ' which we **all** must always be every day of our years on Earth.*

With love, Jeanne

About the Author

Jeanne Halsey is a daughter, sister, wife, mother, grand-mother ... and a writer. Third of five children born to international missionary-evangelist **Dr. Don E. Gossett** and his late wife **Joyce Shackelford Gossett,** Jeanne naturally inherited her father's gift of writing (he has published over 120 books, including the best-selling *"What You Say Is What You Get"* and the ever-popular *"My Never Again List"*). Jeanne was born in Oklahoma ... immigrated to Canada at age 7 ... was educated in British Columbia (*Douglas Junior College, University of British Columbia*) ... and has resided in Oklahoma, Oregon, British Columbia, Washington state, Texas, and Colorado. She has traveled internationally extensively.

Formerly Managing Editor of two internation-ally-distributed monthly Christian magazines, Jeanne is now a freelance writer. She has ghosted and published books for several renown-ed Christian ministries and contemporary person-alities: for her father ... **Reinhard Bonnke** ... **Sarah Bowling** ... **U. Gary Charlwood** ... **Frank Colacurcio** ... **Marilyn Hickey** ... **Kurt Langstraat** ... **Danny Ost** ... **Paul Overstreet** ... **Cliff Self** ... **Robert Tilton** ... **Steve Watt** ... and **many others.** She has written for Christian and secular trade magazines, and has published several Sports articles about National Basketball Association superstar **Luke Ridnour** for *Sports Spectrum* Magazine (a division of *Christianity Today*). She also publishes an Internet newsletter *"e-Jeanne,"* and frequently teaches the *School of Creative Christian Writing,* using her book *"The Legacy of Writing"* as the curriculum.

Jeanne lives in Birch Bay, Washington, with her husband (since 1974) **Kenneth Halsey,** Vice

Jeanne's Extended Family in 2011 (left to right): son-in-law **Patrick Freeman** ... daughter **Jennifer Freeman** ... daughter-in-law **Cherry Halsey**, touching granddaughter **Aja Halsey's** shoulder ... nephew-in-law **Jared Pedersen** ... niece **Vanessa Pedersen** ... niece-in-law **Kelsey Gossett** ... husband **Kenneth Halsey**, holding grandson **Jude Halsey's** shoulder ... nephew-in-law **Brandon Gossett** ... nephew **Jordan Gossett** ... **Jeanne Halsey**, holding granddaughter **Hayley Halsey** in her right arm, and granddaughter **Ava Freeman's** hand ... nephew **Justin Gossett** ... grandson **Kristian Freeman** ... Kristian's girlfriend **Claire Nelson** ... son **Alexander Halsey.** (*Disneyland*, California)

President of Franchise Sales, Western Region, for the *Realogy Corporation;* their empty-nest home includes two purebred Chihuahuas, **Lucia Gracias Royale** and **Juliet Diva Royale**. Their beautiful daughter **Jennifer** is married to **Patrick Freeman;** they have two children, **Kristian** and **Ava;** and thankfully the Freemans live very nearby, in Blaine. Their talented son **Alexander** is married to **Cherry Ruth;** they have three children, **Jude, Aja** and **Hayley;** the younger Halseys live halfway around the world, stationed in India as missionaries with the *Life-Giving Network,* an outreach ministry of *North County Christ the King Church.*

An outspoken activist for Christian causes, Jeanne has stood for public office (she lost); she is past-Chair of the Board of Directors of the *Whatcom County Pregnancy Clinic,* and is past-Secretary of the Board of Directors of the *Greens at Loomis Trail Homeowners Association.* Jeanne and Kenneth are active members of *North County Christ the King Community Church* in Lynden, Washington.

Other Titles

✳ = available through www.lulu.com,
www.amazon.com, or www.halseywrite.com

Non-Fiction

✳ *e-Jeanne: 2003* Once upon a
time (okay, early in 2000), I began
assembling my random musings
(later known as "e-Editorials"),
cutting-and-pasting articles that
interested me, compiling jokes I
thought were funny, and then –
almost on a daily basis – joyfully
spamming my family and friends
through e-mail. This precursor to
now-popular blogs was modestly called *e-Jeanne ...*

✳ *e-Jeanne: 2004 - Part One
(January through July)*
"Once I got started, I couldn't
stop." The history of *e-Jeanne*
began around 1999, really
ramped up when 9/11 hit our
nation, became more
organized and intentional
thereafter, and continued
until ... 2005? ... *e-Jeanne* was
assembled early in the morning (right after my
morning devotions – in fact, I realize many of my
morning devotions somehow crept into the e-
Editorials), and then forwarded by e-mail to over

300 people all around the world. I did this two or three days a week for 10 years. Like I said, maybe I am a little crazy ...

✳ *e-Jeanne: 2004 - Part Two (August through December)* 2004 was a lengthy year, filled with commentary about the impending American Presidential Election (yes, George W. Bush won again), fluctuating health issues, and much sharing of prayer requests and praise reports among the faithful and beloved Readers. 2004 was so long that I had to split it into two books. Like its sister books, *e-Jeanne: 2004 (Part Two)* comes out looking like a fair-sized phone book; you'll need strong arms and strong hands to hold it while reading ... and I strongly suggest you have a sturdy bookmark.

✳ *e-Jeanne Remnants: 2002, 2005, 2008* The final installment in the *e-Jeanne* series, *e-Jeanne Remnants: 2002, 2005, 2008* is the adventure of any ordinary North American woman as she lived through a watershed decade. Packed with humor, confrontation, wisdom, silliness, life and death, health and illness – all the normal components of life), Jeanne Halsey's "online journals" made for interesting reading. *"A must-*

read for anyone interested in real life in North America as told by an honest writer." ~ Gloria Edwards

- ***Exit the Dragon: Fierce Faith Meets Modern Medicine***
- ***Falling Out of the Tower***
- ***International Guard: A New Life Group Initiative***

✷ ***The Legacy of Writing*** An experienced, published writer teaches a Creative Christian Writing Class, using humor, anecdotes and simple facts.

- ***Naked With God***

✷ ***The Parable of Aurelia***
People wonder why Life is so difficult, why it seems we lose more than we gain ... when – despite our best efforts – we are continually diminished by hurts, disappointments, shattered dreams. This parable for the 21st century offers an understanding of why and how God is shaping us for greater purposes than we can even dream!

✳ ***Shame-Free*** How Christian parents can survive their teenager's crisis pregnancy.

✳ ***Stubborn Faith: Celebrating Joyce Gossett*** As we commemorated the 20th year of my mother Joyce Gossett's Homegoing, I want to honor her memory and the incredible legacy she left for me and our entire family. I choose to not forget this remarkable woman of God who changed the world because of her stubborn faith in Jesus Christ.

✳ ***3 Strikes: Dealing With Apathy, Ingratitude and Unbelief*** Apathy, unbelief and ingratitude are three attitudes threatening the Christian Church and undermining the lives of followers of Christ. This book addresses those three sins and offers Bible answers to overturn these failings and walk fresh and strong in Jesus Christ!

✳ *What's That You Have In Your Hands?* Fresh air and hope for the weary soul.

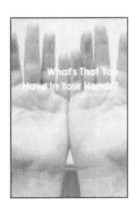

Fiction

✳ *A Bible Fantasy For Jude, Ava, Aja, and Hayley* Four modern-day children are magically trans-ported back to Bible days, where they meet – and play with – Jesus Christ in the middle of the Sea of Galilee ... then hear Him teach the "Sermon on the Mount" ... then share their lunch with Him as He "feeds the 5,000." All from the imagination of gifted writer Jeanne Halsey, and partially illustrated by two of her three granddaughters ... who also star in the story!

✳ *A Christmas Fantasy For Jude and Ava* This is not your run-of-the-mill children's Christmas class. Jeanne "Grammy" Halsey loves to tell stories **to** her

grandchildren ... and **about** her grandchildren! This fantasy – where Jude and Ava magically travel back in time ... meet a mysterious, sweet lady ... and experience the Birth of Jesus Christ – is a tribute to Aunty Judy Gossett, who left this Earth before either her great-nephew or great-niece were even born.

✳ ***And God Created Theatre*** Just as Music and Dance have become commonly accepted forms of Worship in today's Christian Church, I believe it is time to rediscover and reclaim the rightful role of Theatre.

✳ ***Another Chance*** (an Easter Drama) How did Simon Peter genuinely feel during the difficult hours between the arrest, trial, death, and then the resurrection of Jesus Christ? Not yet knowing that Jesus was alive once more, how could he – or anyone – ever expect to have *Another Chance?*

✳ ***Another Christmas Fantasy For Jude, Ava and Aja*** In this sequel to *A Christmas Fantasy for Jude and Ava,* popular writer Jeanne

Halsey adds another grandchild to join in an imaginative adventure back to the time of the birth of Jesus Christ, again aided by a mysterious lady who turns out to be their great-aunt Judy Gossett, who died before any of them were born.

• **Bittersweet** (a Novel of King David and his wife Michel)
• **The Blue Vial** (a Children's Science-Fiction Trilogy)

✳ **Messiah! Bright Morning Star Stage Play,** with Reba Rambo-McGuire and Dony McGuire, William and Gloria Gaither, and Judy A. Gossett The Three Wise Guys (also known as "the Three Wise Men") bumble across to Bethlehem ... Joseph displays new-father jitters ... and Angels eagerly watch from Heaven to see how it all turns out. *Messiah! Bright Morning Star* is a collaboration between noted playwright Jeanne Halsey and award-winning songwriters Reba Rambo and Dony McGuire – a wonderful, humorous musical play!

✳ **Noah's Ark: A Bible Fantasy For Jude, Ava, Aja, Hayley, and Jack and Piper** The greatest art of a Story-Teller is to bring the Reader into the story too, so it often taken "leaps of Faith" to reinvent the world as we know it. What child would not like to imag-ine himself walking up the ramp into Noah's Ark, leading his favor-ite animal? And what child would not like to look up into the sky when Noah points at the rainbow which God has set as a promise, and say in her heart, "That is God's promise for me too"? And what child would not like to pretend to water-ski behind the world's first ocean-liner?

• **That Which I Ought to Do** (a Novel of Paul the Apostle)
• **Ya-Ya** (a Novel of Mary of Bethany)